TALL BUILDINGS OF ASIA & AUSTRALIA

TALL BUILDINGS OF ASIA & AUSTRALIA

Edited by Georges Binder

BUILDINGS OF ASIA & AUSTRALIA

First published in Australia in 2001 by
The Images Publishing Group Pty Ltd
ACN 059 734 431
6 Bastow Place, Mulgrave, Victoria 3170, Australia
Telephone: (613) 9561 5544 Facsimile: (613) 9561 4860
email: books@images.com.au
website: www.imagespublishing.com.au

Tall Buildings of Asia & Australia.

Includes index.
ISBN 1 86470 075 0.

1. Skyscrapers – Asia. 2. Skyscrapers – Australia. 3. Tall buildings – Asia.
4. Tall buildings – Australia 5. Architecture, Modern – 20th century – Asia.
6. Architecture, Modern – 20th century – Australia. I. Binder,
Georges.

720.483095

Designed by The Graphic Image Studio Pty Ltd
Melbourne, Australia
Film by Rainbow Graphics & Printing Co., Ltd.
Printed by Excel Printing Company
Printed in China

Contents

Preface

A. Eugene Kohn
Kohn Pedersen Fox Associates PC

6

The demographic trends of nations and of the major cities of Asia have a great affect on commercial real estate, particularly housing and office buildings. While in Western Europe, Japan, and the United States there is significant increase in its aged population in comparison to people of working age, over one half of the world's population is in Asia, led by China and India with a proportionally smaller aged group. The population is rapidly urbanizing and as a result of political and economic changes of the last couple of decades, there is a great increase in the proportion of office workers. As a result of these demographic trends, the demand for new construction is the greatest in Asia. It is through the tall building that a large portion of the demand for residences and offices will be satisfied.

The initial need as well as the desire to build the tall building in Asia came at a time when the United States was in the midst of a major recession. From the late 1980s to the late 1990s, there was little demand for space. Asia's increased demand however coincided with the availability of United States architects and engineers who already had experience with the design of tall buildings. This outcome was also beneficial for the Asian clients who could now profit from the experience of these firms. For American architects it was not only a time to sharpen skills, but also a chance to develop new concepts, strong forms, and use new and improved materials. In addition to American firms, leading architects with some previous tall building experience from Europe, Japan, Australia, Hong Kong, and throughout Asia joined in the design of the tall building in Asia and their names became more and more identified with outstanding tall buildings, some of which are presented in 'Tall Buildings of Asia and Australia'.

Numerous Asian clients and their architects created the tall building in many cases as a symbol, as a vehicle for expressing their power, importance, and as a tool for attracting international tenants. In addition there was a desire to achieve outstanding, award-winning architecture in cities from Tokyo, Nagoya, Seoul, Singapore, Kuala Lumpur, and Manila to Shanghai; the result however, like in the United States in the mid-1980s, was overbuilding in many Asian cities.

Some Asian clients wanted to exceed the height of the World Trade Center in New York and the Sears Tower in Chicago. Asia now has some new icons with the Jin Mao Tower by Skidmore, Owings & Merrill in Shanghai and the Petronas Towers in Kuala Lumpur by Cesar Pelli. In addition, construction will soon begin on the well-published Shanghai World Financial Center, a Mori building designed by Kohn Pedersen Fox, which will potentially become the world's tallest.

Many of the modern towers recently completed represent advancement in technology and express current aesthetic stylistic trends. The forms, the drama, and the height of these buildings have dominated the approach of the design. In Europe, architecture found solutions that were energy efficient and increasingly environmentally friendly in order to deal with high-energy costs. In Asia, like in the United States however, the majority of the buildings to date have showed less concern for these issues. At the same time efforts have been made, as an example in both Japan and Singapore, to increase efficiency in office buildings through the use of significantly larger floor plates (that is, 5,000 square meters), similar to the United States, and a greater distance from the core to the exterior wall of up to 18 meters.

There is no question that many architectural achievements related to the tall building have appeared from the late 1980s to the late 1990s. They have been made possible by a very hot economy in Asia and Japan, by a strong desire to achieve the new landmark tall buildings, supported by the confidence that demand will continue to grow as a result of continued economic strength. The tall building will be even more popular and many of these Asian cities will be home to the new icons of skyscrapers.

A. Eugene Kohn FAIA RIBA JIA, President
Kohn Pedersen Fox Associates PC
New York, USA

Dennis Lau Wing-kwong
Dennis Lau & Ng Chun Man Architects & Engineers (HK) Limited

Intelligent appraisal of the phenomenon of the tall building demands recognition both of the social and economic forces that shape it and of the architect's role as the agent of those forces. Recent conditions in South East Asia, particularly rapid urbanisation and high land values, have been conducive to the development of tall buildings. Alongside with the steady economic growth since the late 1980s, major Asian cities have seen an intense competition, both internally and amongst each other, in putting up sky-soaring buildings as a sign of prestige and supremacy.

Besides being a symbol of economic culture at the time, high-rise buildings also represent innovation in exploring the use of urban space in all dimensions. As populations continue to converge on the 'nexii' of the prosperity around the world, tall buildings provide a sensible solution for sustaining a high-density development by optimising the use of airspace while relieving more ground floor space for amenity and greenery.

Tall buildings and their visual impact on townscape have often been the subject of repulsion by some planners and environmental preservationists. These criticisms may be founded on a blinkered perception of environmental and cultural values, and defy the evidence of humanity's history of adaptation and the constant flux of urban panoramas. Tall buildings, well-designed, have the potential to facilitate an extremely rich and worthwhile urban environment that mitigates the problems of low-rise urban sprawl.

We consider it incumbent upon us as architects both to invest tall buildings with the same dignity as great buildings of the past and to ensure that they fit comfortably into the existing fabric of cities. The social, intellectual, and commercial aspects of developments in which we aim to add substantial value need not be exclusive however, and indeed have often proved to be complementary when imaginatively approached.

Advance in construction technology is an unavoidable and critical aspect of our work. There is a process of natural selection in which only the most efficient means of building shall prevail at a given time and keeping ahead in this area is a full-time occupation for us. The mechanics of building are, however, only the means to the end in creating a decent, pleasant, and efficient environment and should not be glorified at the expense of the end user.

Dennis Lau Wing-kwong
Dennis Lau & Ng Chun Man Architects & Engineers (HK) Limited
Hong Kong SAR, People's Republic of China

Introduction
By Georges Binder

1

2

3

4

The rise of the Asian and Australian tall building

The 52-story, 178 meter high Connaught Centre [1] (today known as Jardine House), completed in Hong Kong in 1973 and with unusual round windows, is the first real skyscraper that can proudly bear the name in Asia—it was also the tallest in the region at the time of completion.

The history of the Asian high-rise can be traced back to 1935 with the Bank of China [2], Broadway Mansions [3] in Shanghai, and the Hongkong & Shanghai Bank [4] in Hong Kong. The 1948 Jardine House [5] (developed by the company that later developed the Connaught Centre) and the 1950 Bank of China [6], opened the way to a high-rise construction era that made the then British colony one of the few cities in the world, together with Chicago and New York, to develop itself intensively towards the sky.

Over the years many architects have demonstrated their expertise in high-rise design in Asia, however, particular note must be made of Palmer & Turner (today known as P&T Group). Palmer & Turner made their mark on high-rise design in the region by designing all of the above-mentioned projects. It is important to note that during the Second World War Japanese occupation of Hong Kong, all the Palmer & Turner offices were closed; this perhaps explains why the architectural style of immediate post-war projects are similar to pre-war projects, only taller.

There are also Asian tall buildings that did not live long enough to see the new millennium; for example, the Hongkong Hilton [7] completed in 1963. The 283 meter square-shaped, flat-roofed Cheung Kong Center proudly replaced this early Asian international-style tall building in 1999.

Because the earlier earthquake regulations' height limit of 31 meters, Japan did not see a skyscraper until 1968 with the completion of the 36-story Kasumigaseki Building [8] in Tokyo, designed by T. Yamashita Architects & Engineers. However, the first real Japanese skyscraper was the 170 meter, 47-story Keio Plaza Hotel [9] (now Keio Plaza Inter-Continental) completed in 1971 in Tokyo and designed by Nihon Architects, Engineers and Consultants. Located in the Shinjuku area near the Keio Plaza, the 55-story Shinjuku Mitsui Building [10] completed in 1974 and designed by Nihon Sekkei—a firm historically related to the firm that designed the Kasumigaseki Building—definitely established Japan as a place destined to produce more and more major high-rise buildings.

5

6

7

8

Any presentation of early Asian tall buildings would not be complete without mentioning a couple of projects located in Sydney, Australia: these are the AMP Building[11] built in 1962 and designed by Peddle Thorp & Walker, and the 1967 Australia Square[12] designed by Harry Seidler & Associates and structural consultant Pier Luigi Nervi.

The players

Today, Pacific Rim firms such as Architects Pacific, C.Y. Lee & Partners, Dennis Lau & Ng Chun Man Architects & Engineers, Harry Seidler & Associates, Nikken Sekkei, Hijjas Kasturi Associates [13], P&T Group, Rocco Design, T.R. Hamzah & Yeang, Wong & Ouyang, and Wong Tung & Partners, just to name a few, are among the firms that have made their mark in the Asian region. Most of the other major players are American-based architects, including Cesar Pelli & Associates, I.M. Pei & Partners, John Portman & Associates, Kevin Roche John Dinkeloo and Associates, Kohn Pedersen Fox Associates, Murphy/Jahn, and Skidmore, Owings & Merrill, who have all added their Western touch to the design of architecture, very often in context with the local history and culture. In fact, many of the projects produced by these firms are more in context with the local urban fabric than projects produced in their respective countries. This is perhaps due to Asian high-rises, in many instances, finding their inspiration in the local culture, while it is often difficult to differentiate the American from European high-rise designs and vice-versa. There are very few European architectural firms active in the Pacific Rim, and of these the projects designed by Foster and Partners are the most well known. However, firms such as Renzo Piano Building Workshop and Ingenhoven Overdiek und Partner are beginning to bring a European expertise to Australia and China.

The Asian tall building becomes a star

It is probably with Foster's Hongkong & Shanghai Banking Corporation Headquarters[14] (1985) that the fame of an architect working in Asia spread beyond the Asian continent itself and along with it, the fame of Asian architecture. As testament to this, the well-known American architecture magazine 'Progressive Architecture' in March 1986 featured this Hong Kong building as the only major project to be covered in over 40 pages!

1 Connaught Centre (now Jardine House), Hong Kong, Palmer and Turner, 1973 (photograph courtesy P&T Group)
2 Bank of China, Shanghai, Palmer and Turner, 1935 (photograph courtesy P&T Group)
3 Broadway Mansions, Shanghai, Palmer and Turner, 1935 (photograph courtesy P&T Group)
4 Hongkong & Shanghai Bank, Hong Kong, Palmer and Turner, 1935 (photograph courtesy P&T Group)
5 Jardine House, Hong Kong, Palmer and Turner, 1948 (photograph courtesy P&T Group)
6 Bank of China, Hong Kong, Palmer and Turner, 1950 (photograph courtesy P&T Group)
7 Hongkong Hilton, Hong Kong, Palmer and Turner, 1963 (photograph courtesy P&T Group)
8 Kasumigaseki Building, Tokyo, T. Yamashita Architects & Engineers, 1968 (photograph courtesy Nihon Sekkei Inc.)
9 Keio Plaza Hotel (now Keio Plaza Inter-Continental), Tokyo, Nihon Architects, Engineers and Consultants, 1971 (photograph courtesy G. Binder/Buildings & Data s.a.)
10 Shinjuku Mitsui Building, Tokyo, Nihon Sekkei Inc., 1974 (photograph courtesy Nihon Sekkei Inc.)
11 AMP Building, Sydney, Peddle Thorp & Walker Pty Ltd, 1962 (photograph courtesy Peddle Thorp & Walker Pty Ltd)
12 Australia Square, Sydney, Harry Seidler & Associates, 1967 (photograph Max Dupain, courtesy Harry Seidler & Associates)
13 Shahzan Tower, Kuala Lumpur, Hijjas Kasturi Associates, 1990 (photograph courtesy Hijjas Kasturi Associates)
14 Hongkong & Shanghai Banking Corporation, Hong Kong, Foster and Partners, 1985 (photograph Ian Lambot)

A different style of designing and building high-rises

With few exceptions, such as the P&T Group's Entertainment Building (1993) in Hong Kong, the Asian skyline did not see a postmodern era comparable to the United States in the 1980s, nor are there many pre-war high-rises in Asia—the ones that brought the timeless character to the American city. The high-rise buildings found in cities such as Hong Kong, Singapore, and Tokyo are generally designed following a modernist vocabulary, which creates very different skylines to those in the United States. These familiar American skylines remain the reference, but for how long? Other major cities such as Bangkok and Kuala Lumpur have produced projects with more regional imagery. Regardless of the 1997 Asian economy crisis, it is Asia that now leads the world in terms of skyscraper production, just as it has for the last decade.

15

As the American high-rise market takes over again at the beginning of the new century, the market appears to be pushed solely by economic factors and not for the 'ego' reasons that were the driving force for some projects built in the 1980s. The Asian high-rise architecture market, with the exception of Hong Kong, Japan, and Singapore, has possibly not yet acquired this maturity and thus we might continue to see new buildings—some actually quite extraordinary—that respond only partially or perhaps not at all, to the demand of the local economy. It is often the case that 'atypical' buildings are erected by a state, one of its components, or a state-owned company, such as the Jin Mao Building[15] (Skidmore, Owings & Merrill) in Shanghai, or the Petronas Towers[16] (Cesar Pelli & Associates) in Kuala Lumpur. In the case of the 101-story Taipei Financial Center (C.Y. Lee & Partners), the Taiwanese government provided public land. For the countries behind these projects, the main goal is to make their mark rather than exclusively build work or living places required by the market. It must be noted that in terms of image, this trend of erecting super-tall high-rises is successful far beyond the building's local surroundings. Who was talking about Kuala Lumpur before the Petronas Towers were planned, not to mention completed? What would the image of the Pudong zone in Shanghai have been without the Jin Mao Building? These buildings are far more than just buildings: they culturally symbolize cities or countries while at the same time symbolizing the economic activity of a region.

16

The same super-tall 'flagship-like' trend is now under way in the Middle East where three buildings over 300 meters—the 321 meter Burj Al Arab[17] is the new advertised tallest hotel in the world—have recently been completed in Dubai. There are also other high-rise buildings of similar height that are either completed or under planning in that part of the world. In the more conservative Europe, when it comes to the authorization of the construction of high-rises from an urban point of view, it seems that even London may allow some landmark tall high-rises in the central financial district in the near future, while Frankfurt continues to grow vertically as a way to confirm its growing financial power.

15   *Jin Mao Building, Shanghai, Skidmore, Owings & Merrill, 1999*
     (photograph courtesy Grand Hyatt Shanghai)
16   *Petronas Towers, Kuala Lumpur, Cesar Pelli & Associates, 1998*
     (photograph Georges Binder, courtesy Buildings & Data s.a.)
17   *Burj Al Arab, Dubai, W.S. Atkins, 1999 (photograph Georges*
     Binder, courtesy Buildings & Data s.a.)

17

Height, environment, and conclusions

'Tall buildings of Asia & Australia' does not contain a summary of the heights of the world's, Asia's or Australia's tallest buildings. Indeed, what is the value of making comparisons between flat-roofed buildings and buildings with spires and/or masts, despite whether they are television antennae or architectural features? Until the 1990s, there had been few exceptions to the contemporary flat-roofed skyscraper, which allowed for height comparisons. Now, with so many spires and masts atop the tall buildings in Asia, attempting to say which building is 'the tallest' is becoming more and more irrelevant, especially since many buildings have been designed to appear, and actually be, taller than previous ones when counting the tip of their mast or other spire features. But is this really what makes one building taller than the next? As a matter of record, in order to have a full overview of each project, most of the buildings featured in 'Tall Buildings of Asia & Australia' list building details that include the height; however, no comparisons have been made.

An architect who has made Asian designs known far beyond Asia is Ken Yeang from T.R. Hamzah & Yeang—his bio-climatic schemes have been published and presented outside Asia. It is important to note that apart from projects designed by non Asian-architects, very few projects designed by Asian-based architects have been extensively published outside their country of origin. This is in part due to the tall building having been for a long time regarded as a Western product, mainly North American. However, in the near future Asia will probably become the center of the high-rise world, and this may be the case for many years to come. Indeed, despite the 1997 crisis and the relatively short history of the Asian high-rise, Asia has not seen any long-term interruptions to the construction of tall buildings, such as the United States and Canada have seen (1930 to 1955, and, more recently, in the 1990s).

Many Asian high-rise designs definitely have a 'regional' character, especially when compared to most other high-rises that follow a more 'international' style. This makes the Asian high-rise quite unique. 'Tall Buildings of Asia' aims to spread the awareness of projects of outstanding value both due to their intrinsic value and because they represent, more than other buildings elsewhere in the world, a regional character, which is an asset in itself.

A possible question to ponder is: how long will it be before an Asian-based architect designs and builds a major skyscraper in another part of the world?

Georges Binder
Buildings & Data s.a.

TALL BUILDINGS OF ASIA & AUSTRALIA

1063 King's Road

■ Originally occupied by Crown Motors, the site was purchased by Hong Kong Land in 1996. Capitalizing on Quarry Bay's growing reputation as an up-and-coming office district with all the infrastructure—transport, restaurants, and so on—in place, the developer commissioned Wong Tung International Ltd (WTIL) to design a Grade-A office building, the intention being to attract tenants contemplating the relocation of backroom functions from Central.

The architect was keen to increase natural light levels to office spaces thereby reducing dependence on fixed architectural lighting and the heat generated. This means that energy consumption is reduced whilst offering better standards of interior comfort. To achieve this the architect specified low-E glass for this building, and solved the problem of the untidy appearance of desks and partitions being visible from the outside by specifying a low-E tinted glass that would offer all the desired advantages: excellent thermal performance; relatively high levels of natural light transmission; and a smart, uniform external appearance.

Due to site constraints, the 118-space carpark is accommodated in the podium rather than a basement. To overcome the appearance of three levels of carparking above the main entrance, the architect adopted a jumbo louver system consisting of 300 millimeter wide blades set at an angle, which effectively keeps the carpark out of view.

The mechanical floors of the building were also shifted down to the lower floors, so that the office area was pushed up, affording more floors a view over the neighboring buildings. This is expressed by exposed columns on the lower floors, which visually lift the office tower above the carpark podium.

The main entrance, which was notionally shifted to bring it closer to the nearest MTR exit on King's Road, leads into an L-shaped lobby where the sense of spaciousness is enhanced by the use of light-coloured 'statuario venato' marble for the floor and French limestone wall panels with backlit green onyx highlights. About 260 square meters of retail space is also provided on the ground floor.

The core of the building was shifted to the middle of the wall, which abuts an adjacent development in order to maximize the space around the perimeter, so that more areas enjoys natural lighting and views.

1

Location
Hong Kong SAR, People's Republic of China

Completion
November 1999

Height
125 m

Stories
31

Area
Building: 21,600 m²; site: 2,800 m²

Structure
Cast-in-place steel reinforced concrete

Materials
Interpane Ipasol insulated glass; interpane gray-tinted monolithic glass; metal trim: clear/black anodized aluminum; louvers: clear anodized aluminum; stone cladding: polished Sardinia Grey granite and polished/flamed black granite

Use
Offices

Architect
Wong Tung & Partners Limited

Structural engineer
Maunsell Consultants Asia

Services engineer
J. Roger Preston

Client
Hong Kong Land

Contractor
Gammon HK Ltd

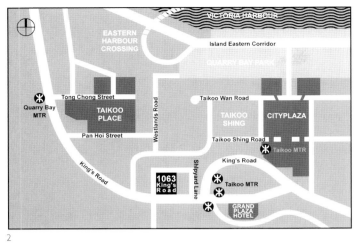

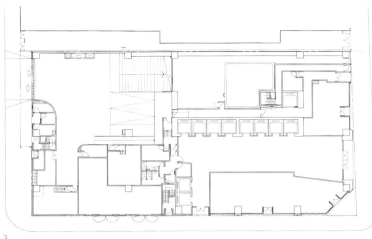

2

3

4

1   View from south
2   Site plan
3   Ground floor plan
4   Main entrance
Photography: courtesy Wong Tung & Partners Limited

208 Wireless Road

■ The design for this office building was done in 1990 with construction completed in 1993. The site is on a portion of Wireless Road immediately adjacent to the Dutch Embassy on one side and the American ambassador's residence on the other.

The architects decided to orient the building's interior spaces to the rear or away from Wireless Road, facing the embassy grounds and affording views of luxurious flora and of the skyline of modern Bangkok.

The developer was required to provide a design that could be separated in the future along the internal lot lines. Hence the building has a low podium on one side and the main tower structure on the other, conforming to the needs of the property owners. The podium was designed for a bank tenant and contains office space on three floors above the ground level, allowing potential tenants to lease large floorplates if required.

The plan of the structure is a direct response to the zoning code of Bangkok. In order to maximize allowable area, the designer needed to closely follow the allowable building perimeter and this has been accomplished on all sides without resorting to the 'wedding cake' designs of many of the buildings in Bangkok.

The elevator and mechanical core is at the front, yielding an entry sequence that intentionally separates the hectic, busy street from the lush, calm interior.

As with many of Architects Pacific's office buildings, the curtain wall is glazed with vision glass from floor to ceiling, except on the sides where punched window openings framed in oversized black aluminum within gray granite walls are provided. The granite sides serve as an indicator of the structure within, wherein support is provided in a rectangular column and shear wall arrangement that on the exterior is expressed with the granite. The glazed portions of the exterior walls reflect the fact that they are not load-bearing.

The entire floor to the rear and to each side is cantilevered from the core, allowing for both flexibility in office layouts and efficient parking floors. On a site as oddly shaped and tight as this, with restrictions as to future ownership of the two parcels, provision of parking was a major concern. The need to eliminate as many columns as possible and locate them optimally with regard to parking dimension requirements as opposed to office module needs, in many ways dictated the structural solution which in turn influenced the planning of the floors.

Location
Bangkok, Thailand

Completion
June 1995

Height
Building: 68.10 m; overall: 76.80 m

Stories
17

Structure
Reinforced concrete

Use
Offices

Architect
Architects Pacific

Associate architect
Ongsa Architect Co. Ltd

Structural engineer
Meinhardt, Hong Kong

MEP engineer
Meinhardt, Hong Kong

Client/Owner
Euromill Development

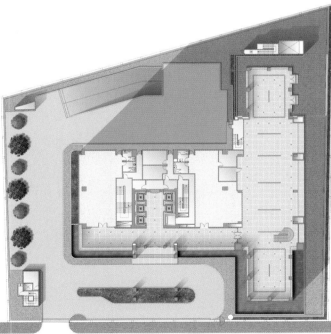

2

3

4

1   South elevation
2   Floor type diffuser
3   Corner detail of curtain wall
4   Site plan
5   Entrance/drop-off area
Photography: courtesy Architects Pacific

5

Baiyoke Sky Hotel

■ In 1983, the first Baiyoke Tower project started with the intention of being the highest building in Thailand and the landmark for the largest wholesale garments export center. When completed in 1987, its rainbow color immediately became the 'talk of the town', together with the gable structure frame rooftop, representing Thailand's tallest tower for more than 10 years.

The success of the Baiyoke Tower initiated the Baiyoke Tower II project in 1988. Having the silhouette of the first Baiyoke Tower as its base, Baiyoke Tower II stands tallest with its red sandstone massive concrete base, giving the image of natural sandstone rising from the earth, punched out to provide space for humans' various activities. The higher it goes, the more modernized and sophisticated these various voids become.

The glittering gold color, a Thai/oriental element symbolizing wealth, defines the top silhouette of Baiyoke I that points upward to the top of Baiyoke II: a suggestion of continuous prosperity.

The Baiyoke Towers I and II are situated in the heart of Pratunam, a long-established wholesale garments market of Bangkok that has become an export center. The surrounding sites are mostly low-rise high-density shophouses of the old business sectors with which the Baiyoke Towers have smoothly blended. Nowadays, the 'Baiyoke' Towers have become Bangkok's landmark in its own right. It still is and shall be the highest building in Thailand for a long time to come.

2

1

3

Location
Bangkok, Thailand

Completion
June 1999

Height
309 m (excluding antenna)

Stories
88 and 2 underground

Area
172,000 m²

Structure
Reinforced concrete

Use
Hotel and commercial

Cost
3,400 million Baht

Architect
Plan Architect Co. Ltd, Plan Associates Co. Ltd, Plan Studio Co. Ltd

Structural engineer
Arun Chaiseri Consulting Engineers Co. Ltd

System engineer
W. and Associates Consultant Co. Ltd

Construction management
Project Planning Service Co. Ltd

Client
Land Development Co. Ltd

General contractor
Concrete Constructions (Thailand) Co. Ltd

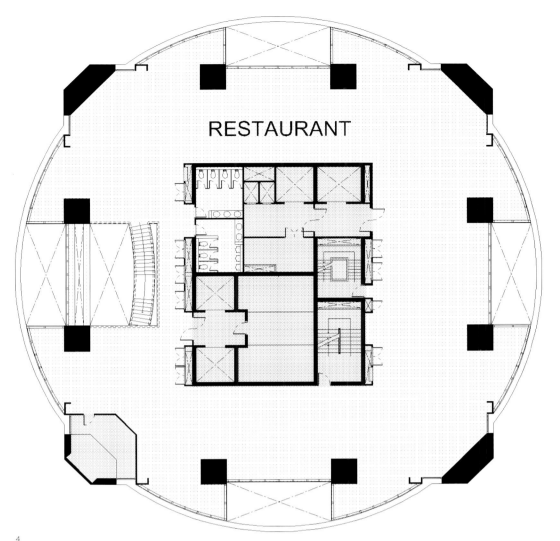

RESTAURANT

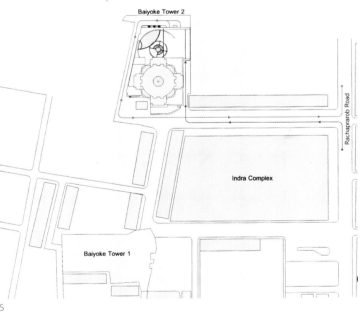

Baiyoke Tower 2

Rachaprarob Road

Indra Complex

Baiyoke Tower 1

1 Interior of Sky Restaurant 2
2 View from north
3 View from east
4 Seventy-forth–eightieth floor plan
5 Site plan
6 Interior of Sky Restaurant 1
Photography: Mr Piphat Phattanathavorn

Beijing China Resources Building

■ The general layout and the main tower of this project are evenly balanced and magnificently characterized. The rectangular tower is placed in the middle of a podium that is in a U-shape surrounding the entrance. Trees have been planted around the courtyard. The tower is decorated with granite and glass. The central metal part is joined with the transparent glass body. Granite fins have been highlighted on the tower's elevations giving an elegant and vertical grace to the building. Fins are extended from the ground all the way to roof level —these further strengthen the grandeur of the architectural work.

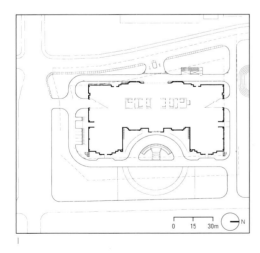

1

2

Location
Beijing, People's Republic of China

Completion
1999

Height
100 m

Stories
26 and 3 underground

Area
Building: 71,000 m²; site: 13,000 m²

Structure
Tube frame structure with box foundation

Materials
Interior: stone, carpet, metal ceiling panel; exterior: stone, aluminum fin/frame, green low-reflection transparent glass

Use
Offices

Cost
710 million RMB

Architect
HOK International (Asia/Pacific) Ltd; Architecture Design Institute Ministry of Construction

Client
China Resources Building Co. Ltd

Contractor
China Construction 1st Division Group Company Ltd

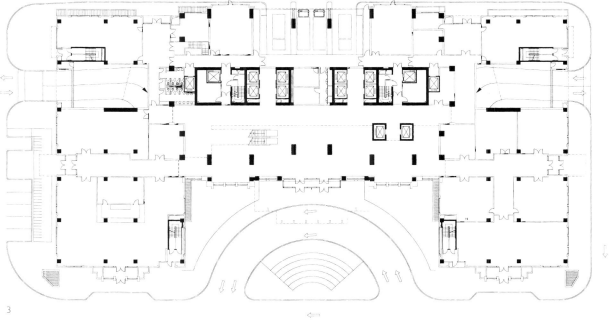

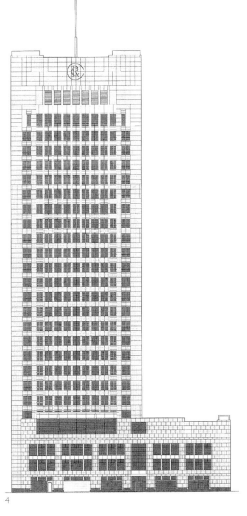

1   Site plan
2   Whole view
3   Ground floor plan
4   South elevation
5   East elevation
Photography: courtesy of Architecture Design Institute Ministry
of Construction

Beijing Jianhong Building

■ This project is situated at the Bai Jia Zhuang Dong Li of the Chao Yang District of Beijing. The project is composed of three apartment towers that are facing the Tuan Jie Hu Park. It has residential communities on both east and west sides. The first and second floors of the podium are a department store; the third floor is designed to have a restaurant and an entertainment center. The floors above are apartments. The three blocks are placed so they all have good orientation, ventilation, and views of the park. The two main entrances of the store have been decorated with modern materials and techniques for the purpose of architectural modeling. An excellent national style of modeling has been adopted called a 'cloud wall', which is traditionally used in residences and gardens. It is in these ways that the architect has made the building appear novel, imposing, and elegant.

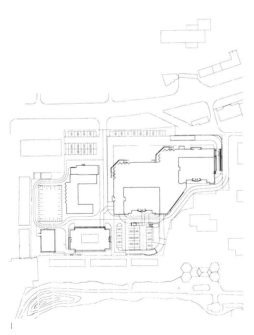

1

2

Location
Beijing, People's Republic of China

Completion
April 2000

Height
93.05 m

Stories
26

Area
Building: 87,300 m²; site: 17,900 m²

Structure
Frame shear wall

Materials
Interior: stone, carpet, emulsion paint, timber flooring; exterior: stone, tile, curtain wall, aluminum window/door

Use
Offices; apartments; food and beverage outlets; entertainment facilities

Cost
310 million RMB

Architect
Architecture Design Institute Ministry of Construction

Client
Beijing Jianhong Real Estate Development Co. Ltd

Contractor
Beijing Urban Construction 5th Construction Co. Ltd

3

4

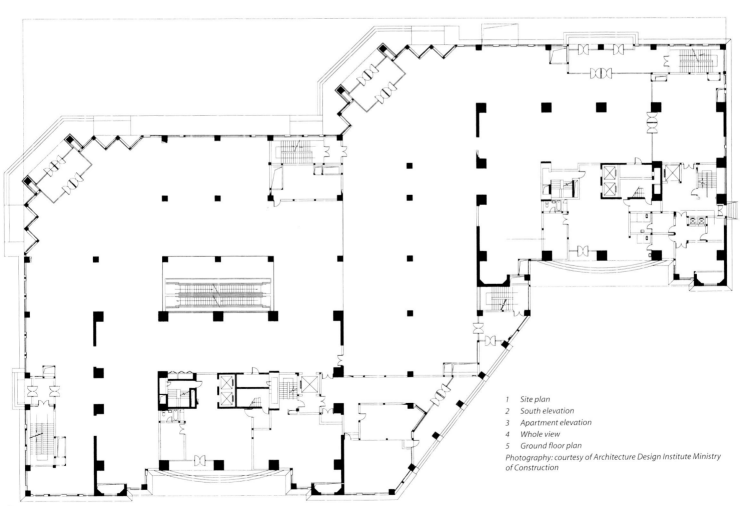

5

1   Site plan
2   South elevation
3   Apartment elevation
4   Whole view
5   Ground floor plan

Photography: courtesy of Architecture Design Institute Ministry of Construction

Beijing Silver Tower

■ Beijing is a fast-developing city that has become increasingly cosmopolitan and modernized. At the same time, it is the capital of the country and has several past dynasties; this creates a strong cultural background with an intense historical heritage and tradition. Any new development in this city ought therefore make a reference to the essence of China's heritage. Silver Tower is in every respect a modern building in its function and facilities, and its image is contemporary. But within its contemporary form, the following aspects of traditional Chinese architecture are embodied:

Precision and ordered organization

Precision and order are the main characteristics of traditional Chinese architecture, such as the post-beam construction methodology and window and door panel modules. In fact, a modular approach was adopted very early on in Chinese architecture. The same principle of precision and order is reflected in Silver Tower's organization and expression.

Honesty and frugality of expression

Apart from certain special building types such as palaces, temples, and so on, traditional architecture, such as domestic buildings, were honest and direct, free from unnecessary adornment.

Form-function relationship

The unique forms of traditional Chinese architecture are mostly derived from functional needs. The courtyard house, for instance, is a response to the life-pattern of large families. The large pitched roofs are a protection against rain and weather. The unique roof bracket construction is a technical solution to produce a large enough cantilever to support the large roof. While most of these features are no longer relevant to modern construction, the concept of form evolving from function remains valid. In the Silver Tower, the form is derived from the context and the different functional needs: sun-shading provision, vertical transportation provision, and so on, which all contribute to the visual image of the architecture.

The design of the Silver Tower integrates modern requirements with the traditional characteristics. The two curved façades not only respond to its context but also represent modernity. The surface of the more rectangular façades employ different sizes of square pattern to pay homage to traditional expression, but at the same time, the three-dimensional square pattern is also acting as a sun-shading device to minimize solar gain and glare—a necessary element to reduce energy consumption.

1

Location
Beijing, People's Republic of China

Completion
1997

Height
145 m with mast; 125 m without mast

Stories
32

Area
66,200 m²

Structure
Reinforced concrete with structural steel for top three floors

Materials
Exterior: glass and aluminum curtain wall; interior: granite floor and wall, aluminum-panel wall and ceiling

Use
Commercial

Cost
HK$400 million

Architect
Rocco Design Ltd

Associate Architect
Architecture Design Institute Ministry of Construction

Structural engineer
Architecture Design Institute Ministry of Construction

Electrical/Mechanical consultant
Rocco Design Ltd and Architecture Design Institute Ministry of Construction

Client
Beijing Silver Tower Real Estate Development Co. Ltd

Contractor
Beijing First Zhong Jian Construction Co.

2

3

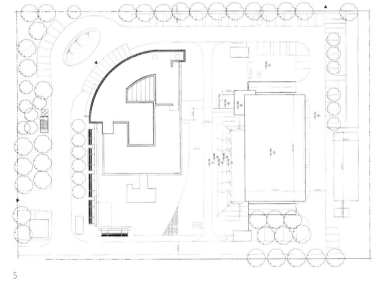

5

4

1   Exterior view
2   Façade and canopy details
3   Main lobby (sculpture by Bernard Venet)
4   Façade details
5   Site plan
6   Typical floor plan
Photography: courtesy Rocco Design Ltd

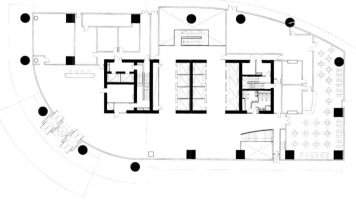

6

BNI City

■ Zeidler Roberts Partnership was retained as master-planner for this mixed-use superblock development situated on a 15 hectare site in central Jakarta. The firm is also the design architect for the 46-story office tower, Wisma 46, presently the tallest structure in Indonesia, located on a 3 hectare site within the development.

With its distinguished roof mast, granite, and reflective curtain wall exterior, this office building is the most distinguished landmark on the Jakarta skyline. Components of the master plan also include the existing Bank Negara Indonesia Headquarters Building, a 716-room prestige hotel, and future residential and commercial development.

The 46-story edifice, the tallest in Jakarta, is symbolic of the year the BNI bank was founded: 1946. The basic floor plate for each tower is 1,672 square metres, laid out to incorporate the latest thinking of a progressive North American office tower. Despite the seemingly complex form of the tower, most of the floor plates are basically rectangular with a slight curve to the north and south sides. The window to core distance of 13.5 meters allows an efficient subdivision of each floor plate. The elevator core is divided into low-, mid-, and high-rise sections, with 18 elevators, an executive elevator serving selected floors, and a service elevator serving all floors. Separate parking elevators connect to the parking garage.

The office tower was designed as an intelligent building, incorporating advanced technological features that provide the most efficient and functional office building in Jakarta.

The tower itself has a distinct sculptural form that has become a landmark in the skyline of Jakarta. The tower appears to have a glass body held on the south and north sides by slightly curved granite walls. Its top protrudes sail-like above those walls, recalling the image of the bank's logo. The granite walls, perforated by a series of windows, accentuate the slimness and height of the tower. The screen-like quality of the walls, clearly visible as edges, is further enhanced by the stepping-back of the tower form towards the top, leaving the upper windows in the walls open to the sky. The exterior form of the tower is the most predominant element on the site and clearly visible from all sides, particularly from the south entrance road. The color of stone cladding of the tower harmonizes with the beige-gray color of the cladding on the existing BNI building.

1

Location
Jakarta, Indonesia

Completion
May 1996 (office tower)

Height
250 m with mast, 228 m without mast

Stories
46 (plus additional skyloft level)

Area
Floor: 140,028 m²

Structure
Reinforced concrete

Materials
Granite, glass curtain wall, aluminum

Use
Commercial

Design architect and master planner
Zeidler Roberts Partnership/Architects

Project architect (office tower)
DP Architects PTE

Structural engineer
T.Y. Lin South-East Asia Pte Ltd

Mechanical and electrical engineer
Ewbank Preece Engineers Pte Ltd

Client
PT Lyman Investindo

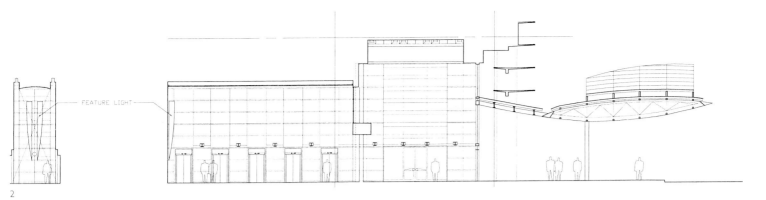

2

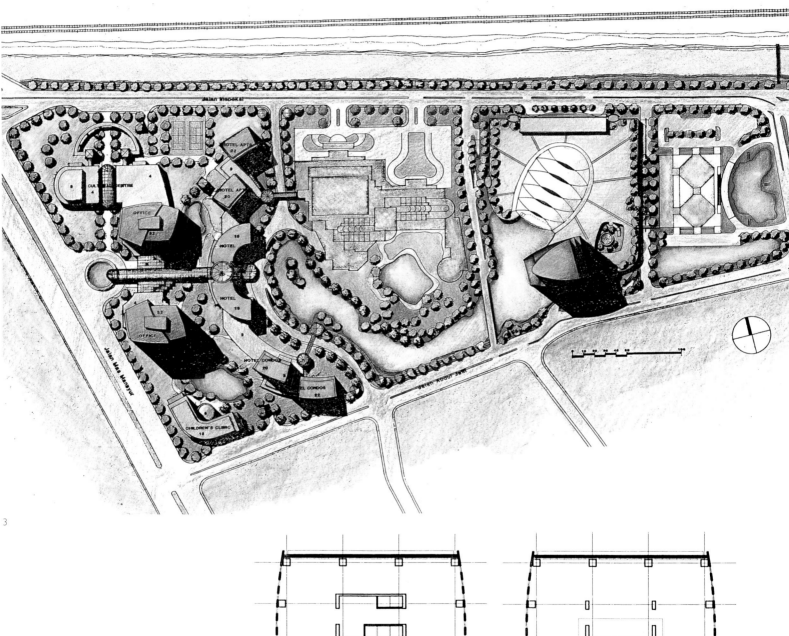

3

1   With its distinguished roof mast, granite, and reflective curtain
    wall exterior, this 46-story office building is the most
    distinguished landmark on the Jakarta skyline
2   Elevator and main lobby elevations
3   Master plan proposal
4   Twenty-seventh level floor plan
5   Thirtieth level floor plan
Photography: courtesy Zeidler Roberts Partnership/Architects

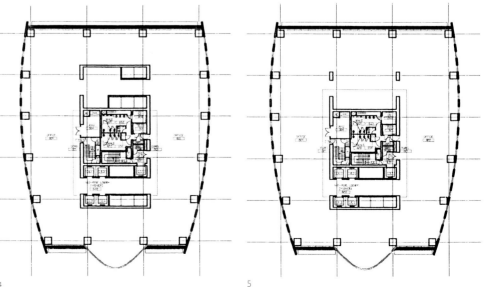

4   5

Capital Square

■ In the heart of Kuala Lumpur's central business district, on a 6.15 hectare parcel, Multi-Purpose Management proposed to build one of the largest integrated mixed-use urban developments in Malaysia.

The master plan by John Portman & Associates integrates a complex program of office, hotel, and conference facilities, retail, parking, and luxury residences all integrated on an urban site. By phasing its components and designing for local climate, culture, and the construction technology of the region, the team has created a dynamic commercial center with the intent of providing festive visibility and exposure for office and retail tenants. The retail component for example is based on the concept of a galleria and atrium. A series of connecting atria, between the four 'compartments' of the centre, act as unifying elements and orient visitors within the centre. Parking, delivered in Phase I with the first office building, will also service the retail centre and becomes a shared amenity integrating the site.

While providing the owner the flexibility of a phased development, the initiation of this project introduced Phase I, which was driven by smart economics of the time and a regional demand for office facilities. Phase I is a new, 40-story office tower clad in stone, glass, and a regionally responsive aluminum sunscreen. This 65,030 square meter tower, with associated underground parking, has created a successful start to the mixed-use complex. Phase II is scheduled to introduce an upscale, retail shopping center, a second office tower, and high-rise luxury condominium towers.

1

2

Location
Kuala Lumpur, Malaysia
Completion date
1989
Stories
40
Area
Building: 65,030 m²
Structure
Reinforced concrete

Materials
Stone, glass, aluminum sunscreen
Use
Office, residential, hotel, retail, parking
Architect
John Portman & Associates
Associate architect
Jurubena Bertiga International Sdn
Structural engineer
T.Y. Lin & Associates

Service engineer
ICB Sdn Bhd
Client
Capital Square Sdn Bhd
Contractor
Bandar Raya Development Construction Sdn Bhd

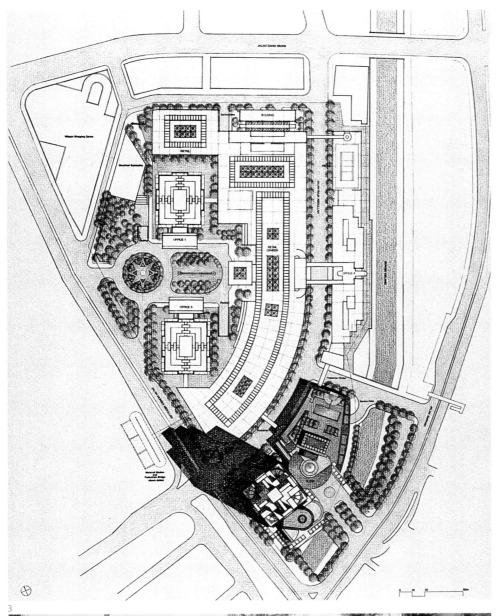

3

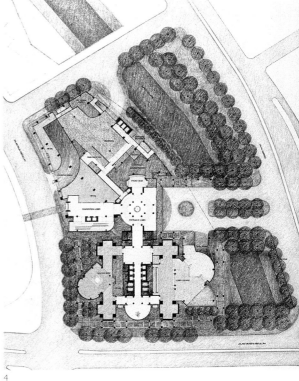

4

5

6

1   View of ultimate build-out with twin 40-story office towers
    in left foreground and hotel at right
2   Phase I office tower, looking north
3   Master plan
4   Hotel site plan
5   Phase I office tower entry court looking northwest
6   Phase I office tower, view of main entrance looking northeast

Photography: courtesy Michael Portman/John Portman &
Associates

Capital Tower

■ Prominently located at the junction of Cecil Street, Maxwell Road, and Robinson Road, Capital Tower emerges as a visual signifier marking the southern extent of the financial district. Capital Tower is a Grade A prime office building that will meaningfully contribute towards the continuing realization of the Singapore downtown as a financial hub of international prominence.

The site is bounded by Cecil Street and Robinson Road on its northwest and northeast peripheries with an open urban space occupying the southern apex and Capital Tower on the north. The site organization essentially emerged from the guidelines and constraints of various authorities. The relative positioning of the park and the building, including the limits of the high-rise and low-rise components within the building, are as per the Urban Redevelopment Authority's zoning guidelines. Likewise, the Mass Rapid Transit (MRT) reserve line indicated by the Mass Rapid Transit Corporation (MRTC) has a strong bearing on the actual positioning of the building.

The design approach was based on a process of integration—the integration of programmatic functions of the tower and the urban plaza into one unified complex and the integration of the complex into the city fabric. The realization of this vision ensures that the urban plaza is neither an isolated retreat nor merely a theatrical forecourt for the tower. Instead, with its eye-catching water feature, it has emerged as an active component of the green belt along Maxwell Road and Capital Tower.

The interweaving of programmatic functions typically associated with a park with functions typical of an office building has the advantage of fostering greater human interaction and creativity. The amalgamation of formal zones of work with the informal zones of recreation helps to alleviate work-related stress and enhance productivity. The gesture strengthens the perception of 'working in a park'.

The design approach was adopted to generate a scheme that is in a state of equilibrium with its context yet remaining conducive to the creation of a stately landmark—a significant object against the backdrop of the sky.

Location
Singapore, Republic of Singapore

Completion
June 2000

Height
256 m

Stories
52 and 1 basement

Area
Floor: 95,556 m²; site: 7,110 m²

Use
Offices

Architect
RSP Architects Planners & Engineers (Pte) Ltd

Structural engineer
Maunsell Consultants (S) Pte Ltd

Mechanical and electrical engineer
Parsons Brinckerhoff Consultants Pte Ltd

Client
Pidemco Land Limited

Contractor
Sangyong Engineering & Construction Co.

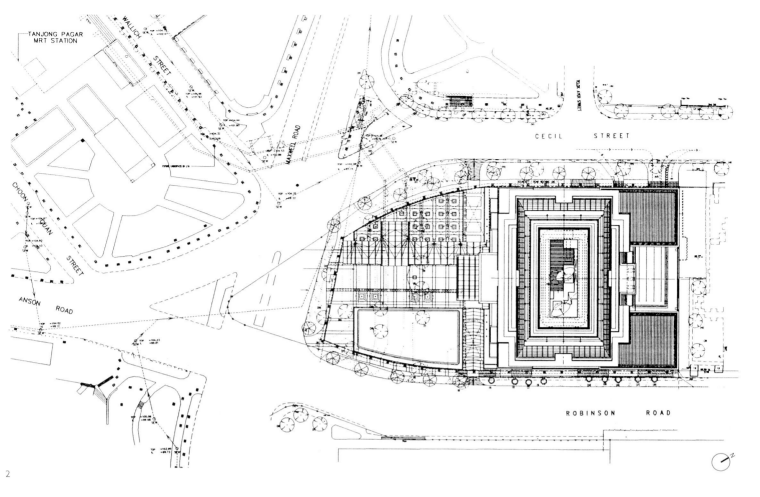

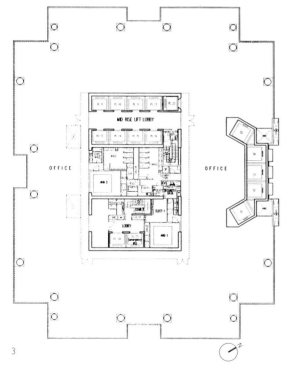

1   Model of Capital Tower
2   Location plan
3   Typical office layout plan
4   View of tower from urban plaza
Photography: courtesy RSP Architects Planners & Engineers (Pte) Ltd

The Center

■ This 73-story towering office building was conceived as a glimmering urban sculpture embracing the most up-to-date intelligent office environment and to meet changing needs at the turn of the century. Considering the height restriction and the extremely enclosed site, the intertwined square floor plate arrangement offers the best solution to floor efficiency and tenants' prospects, and maintains a comfortable distance from other existing buildings that surround the site.

At the street level, the design gives strong recognition to the absolute shortage of open space in the western part of central Hong Kong, and to the existing chaotic traffic condition—a pleasant and safe pedestrian zone is created by elevating the tower about 15 meters above ground as a dedication to the community providing 'breathing space' and public passage in the midst of the concrete jungle. Landscaping to some open space was done in a contemporary Chinese style to recapture the lane character, as well as giving due respect to the history of the place.

1

2

Location
Hong Kong SAR, People's Republic of China

Completion
Mid-1998

Height
346 m (to top of tower mast); 302 m (to top of roof)

Stories
73

Area
Site: 8,816 m²; gross floor area: 130,032 m²

Structure
Steel-framed construction

Materials
Glass, stainless steel, and granite

Use
Offices and commercial

Cost
US$384.6 million

Architect
Dennis Lau & Ng Chun Man Architects & Engineers (HK) Ltd

Building services engineer
Associated Consulting Engineer

Structural consultant
Maunsell Consultants Asia Ltd

Geotechnical engineer
Maunsell Geotechnical Services Ltd

Main contractor
Paul Y – ITC

Developer
Land Development Corporation and Cheung Kong (Holdings) Ltd

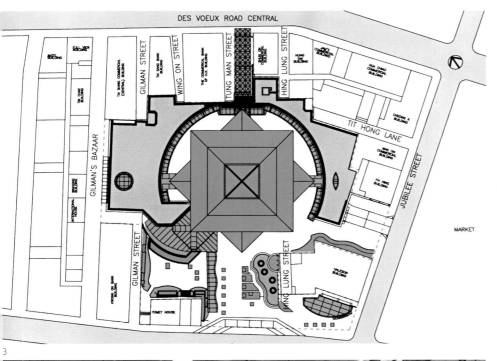

3

4

5

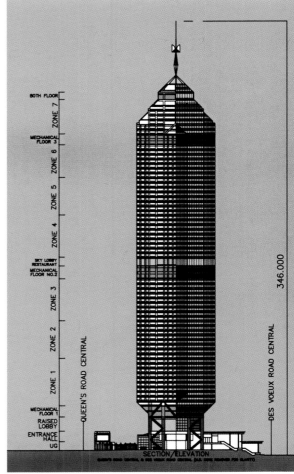

6

1 Pedestrian plaza below office tower
2 View from Queen's Road Central
3 Site plan
4 Night view from Sheung Wan
5 Raised office lobby at sixth floor
6 Section and elevation
Photography: Frankie Wong & Michael Tse Photography

Central Plaza

■ Central Plaza, the 78-story office tower developed at the Wanchai Seafront, is the tallest office building in Hong Kong. Rising to a height of 309.4 meters to the top of the building and 373.9 meters to the pinnacle of the mast—which is an integral part of the building—the structure stands as one of the tallest in Asia.

Elegantly designed in the form of a sleek triangular pillar, the tower has a pyramidal roof with a 60 meter tall mast at the top. At night it is outlined by gold neon light and optical-quality floodlighting, while the glass pyramid at the roof glows with different colored lights.

The building adds a whole new dimension to high-class office properties by offering its tenants the finest leisure facilities. In addition to a swimming pool at the podium garden, there is a deluxe tenants' club equipped with food and beverage outlets, and a full range of recreational and meeting facilities.

1

2

Location
Hong Kong SAR, People's Republic of China

Completion
October 1992

Height
373.9 m (to top of tower mast); 309.4 m (to top of roof)

Stories
78

Area
Site: 7,230 m²; gross floor area: 130,140 m²

Structure
Reinforced concrete

Materials
Interior: natural granite and sandstone cladding; exterior: curtain wall and natural granite cladding

Use
Commercial

Cost
US$141 million

Architect
Dennis Lau & Ng Chun Man Architects & Engineers (HK) Ltd (originally known as Ng Chun Man & Associates Architects & Engineers (HK) Ltd)

Structural engineer
Ove Arup & Partners HK Ltd

Electrical and mechanical engineer
Associated Consulting Engineer

Main contractor
Manloze Ltd

Developers
Sun Hung Kai, Sino Land, Ryoden

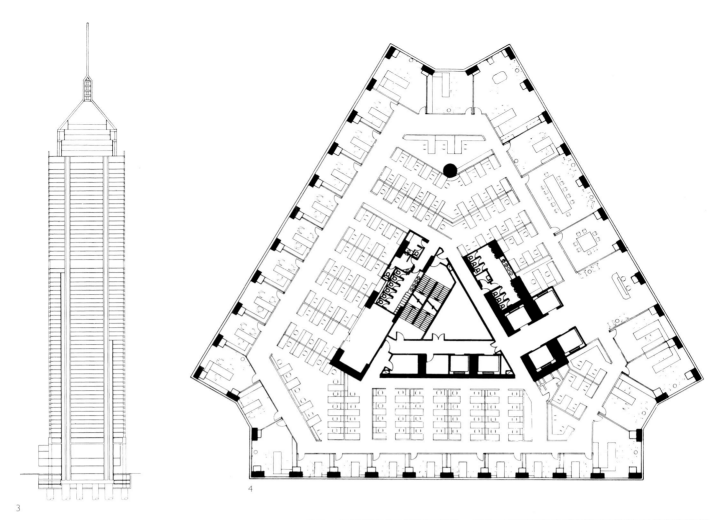

3

4

5

6

7

8

1   Internal feature column at first floor pedestrian concourse
2   View from Kowloon side with neon light features turned on
    at dusk
3   Section
4   High zone office plan
5   View from Causeway Bay
6   Glass wall detail at ground floor main entrance
7   Ground floor main entrance
8   Site plan
Photography: Frankie Wong & Michael Tse Photography

Central Plaza

■ The typical office floor in this 'wafer-thin' tall building is column free (as a marketing requirement of the client). To enable this, structural cross-bracing is provided at the end of the columns of the east and west façades.

Vertical planting steps up diagonally along the north face of the building up to the pool side at the top of the building. A system of louvers and balconies are located on the hot west façade. The core, which consists of a lift lobby, stairways, and toilets, has natural ventilation and natural lighting.

A curved fully glazed curtain wall on the north face gives an uninterrupted view of the distant hills. As this face does not receive direct solar insulation, its sunshade-free elevation becomes a form of geographical indication of the northerly direction. The east and west glazing is recessed from the structure for sun shading. The main staircase, toilets, lift lobbies, and ground-floor lobby are all naturally ventilated.

1

2

Location
Kuala Lumpur, Malaysia

Completion
June 1996

Height
109.6 m

Stories
27

Area
2,982.5 m²

Structure
Reinforced concrete structural frame with prestressed beams, brick infill

Materials
External: laminated float glass, solid aluminum cladding

Use
Office

Architect
T.R. Hamzah & Yeang Sdn Bhd

C&S engineer
Reka Perunding Sdn Bhd

M&E enginer
Jurutera Perunding LC Sdn Bhd

Client
Malview Sdn Bhd

Contractor
Kemas Construction Sdn Bhd

3

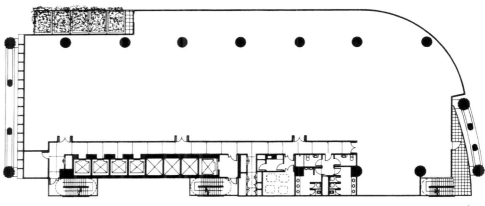

4

5

1   Site plan
2   West elevation
3   Lift lobby
4   Typical floor plan
5   Detail showing entrance canopy
Photography: T.R. Hamzah & Yeang Sdn Bhd

Central Plaza One and Two

■ Central Plaza is a dual tower commercial development located in the financial heart of Brisbane. It is a striking example of contemporary architecture, which incorporates the latest developments in technology and construction to provide tenants with a sophisticated working environment.

Central Plaza One is the taller of the two buildings. Its tower has a square plan form with one corner truncated at ground level. The plan of the building changes shape from a five-sided structure at ground level to an eight-sided structure at roof level. Attached to the northeastern side of the tower is a six-story bank annexe.

The concept envisaged a sleek tower, inspired by the pure form of a crystal. The prismatic forms have been detailed to reflect the sharp edges and simple shapes of this crystaline shaft idea.

Central Plaza Two complements Central Plaza One by the retention of the taller building's uncluttered roof-lines and crisp, clean façade. The shorter building has been designed to maximize the site's potential and accordingly Central Plaza Two has a floor plate approximately 30 percent larger than Central Plaza One.

Both buildings have building maintenance units designed to minimize adverse impact on their uncluttered roof lines. The unit on Central Plaza Two follows the perimeter of the roof, climbing the steep slopes as it does so. However, it was not possible to utilize the Central Plaza Two arrangement on Central Plaza One due to the changing configuration of the latter building's floor plan. The unit adopted for Central Plaza One is both dynamic and innovative, and when in use it creates another dimension to Brisbane's tallest building.

The top 3.27 meters of the roof of Central Plaza One is formed by a horizontal crane jib that lifts and rotates. The building maintenance cage is located on the northeastern end of the jib and exits the corner of the building through secret doors in the façade. By a predetermined series of computer commands, the cage is aligned parallel to the building's façades thereby facilitating maintenance.

1

Location
Brisbane, Australia

Completion
Plaza One: June 1988; Plaza Two: March 1989

Height
Plaza One: 181 m; Plaza Two: 113.55 m

Stories
Plaza One: 47; Plaza Two: 28

Area
Plaza One: building (including basements): 65,450 m²; floor: 1,350 m²; Plaza Two: building (including basements): 51.179 m²; floor: 1,706 m²

Materials
Curtain wall: aluminum sheet with off-white PVF₂ coating; silver-blue laminated reflective glass; roof: profiled aluminum louvers mounted vertically and finished with off-white PVF₂ coating

Architects in association
Peddle Thorp & Harvey (Brisbane); Peddle Thorp & Walker (Sydney); Kisho Kurokawa Architect & Associates (Japan)

Structural engineer
Plaza One: Maunsell and Partners; Plaza Two: Connell Wagner

Mechanical engineer
Norman Disney and Young

Electrical engineer
Lincolne Scott Australia

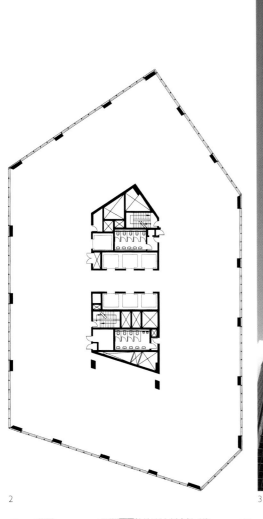

2

3

4

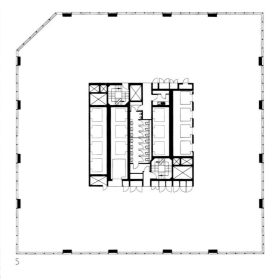

5

Hydraulics engineer
Plaza One: Ledingham Hensby & Oxley;
Plaza Two: Funnell Hydraulics Consultancy

Developer
Land Equity Corporation

Owner
AXA and Queensland Investment Corporation

Contractor
Plaza One: Thiess Watkins White Group;
Plaza Two: Concrete Constructions

1   Plaza One and Two model
2   Plaza Two, high-rise floor plan
3   View from corner of Elizabeth and Creek streets
4   Plaza One foyer
5   Plaza One, low-rise floor plan
Photography: Paul Torcello and Peddle Thorp & Walker Pty Ltd

■ Located in the Lujiazui finance and trade zone of the Pudong area of Shanghai, the China Insurance Building was selected as the winning scheme of an international design competition.

The unique qualities of the building are derived from the marriage of the cylindrical forms with the orthogonal geometric form into a powerful sculptural composition, which is readily identifiable both at pedestrian and rooftop level. The twin circular forms are introduced at the podium level and emerge from the base to create the tower configuration. The mass of the tower is refined in steps as it reaches the upper floors, to be ultimately expressed as pure cylinders topped by twin spires. This culminates with twin beacons and slender mast structures at roof level. The rooftop silhouette provides the China Insurance Building with a strong, unique symbol, identifying the project in the city fabric and on the skyline. At night the rooftop towers become twin beacons of light and reinforce the building's characteristic signature.

The podium is expressed as a series of cascading forms complete with terraces and skylights, and encloses a conference center, recreational facilities, retail and restaurant facilities, and a two-story banking hall. The 12 meter high banking hall has two mezzanine levels with direct escalator access from the building lobby. Three below-grade levels provide parking for 260 cars, as well as building service spaces.

Materials selected for the project reinforce the smooth lines of the cylindrical forms. Blue-tinted glass is combined with silver metal panels to create a sparkling, contemporary image. Podium levels feature light gray granite cladding in combination with metal and glass. Plazas incorporate two contrasting shades of granite, and paving patterns reinforce the overall design concept.

The soaring four-story lobby expresses the intersection of the vertical shaft of the tower and the horizontal terracing of the podium. This duality is prominent in the treatment of the space as a volume. The grand lobby is pierced by solid granite core elements that are bridged by light metal and glass infill elements. The transparency of the four-story glazed exterior wall is emphasized as light penetrates through the full-height volume. Stainless steel horizontal fin bands are carried throughout the interior as scored patterns on the granite, metal, and glass surfaces.

1

Location
Shanghai, People's Republic of China

Completion
1999

Height
196 m to top of spire

Stories
38 (4-story podium with 34 office floors)

Area
Site: 7,263 m²; building: 62,000 m²

Structure
Reinforced concrete

Materials
Exterior: glass curtain wall with metal spandrel panels, and granite panels around podium; interior: polished granite and stainless steel accents (lobbies)

Use
Offices; podium uses include: conference center, recreational facilities, retail areas, restaurant, and banking hall

Cost
US$80 million

Architect
WZMH Architects (design phases)

Associate architect
East China Architectural Design and Research Institute (working drawings and construction phases)

Structural engineer
Quinn Dressel & Associates

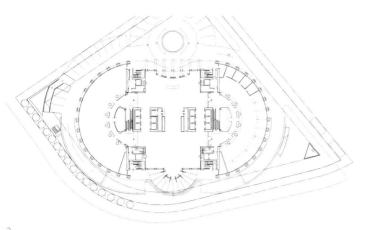

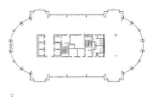

3

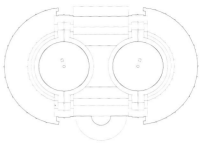

4

2

5

Mechanical engineer
The Mitchell Partnership

Electrical engineer
Mulvey+Banani International Inc.

Client
People's Insurance Company of China

Contractor
Shanghai No. 1 Construction Company

1   Perspective view
2   Site plan and ground floor plan
3   Levels thirty seven–thirty eight
4   Roof level
5   Lobby
Photography: courtesy WZMH Architects

China Merchants Tower

■ The China Merchants Tower, a 39-story high-rise in Pudong, is one of Shanghai's premiere office locations and major architectural landmarks. With a total floor area of approximately 58,400 square meters and a plot ratio of 8, the distinctively striated tower commands prime views of the entire metropolitan area.

The symbolically charged building form, a cylinder within a rectangular volume, derives from overlaying the Chinese symbols for heaven (a circle) and earth (a square). The resultant typical plan readily accommodates the practical requirements of a modern office tower.

The central core serves flexible work levels that can be organized as modular zones. A five-story lobby atrium with dual main entries is clad with aluminum panels that echo treatment of the exterior skin at street level. Elsewhere, marble wall and floor panels conjoin in simple geometric rhythms that establish a tangible corporate ambiance. Contrasting materials, textures, and lighting conditions further reinforce the accomplishment of professional tasks.

1

Location
Shanghai, People's Republic of China

Completion
1995

Height
140 m

Stories
39

Area
Site: 7,301 m²; floor: 58,408 m²

Structure
Reinforced concrete/beam and column

Materials
Curtain wall: glass and aluminum panels

Use
Offices

Cost
HK$540 million

Architect
Simon Kwan & Associates Ltd

Service engineer
Parsons Brinckerhoff Asia Ltd

Client
China Merchants Group

2

3

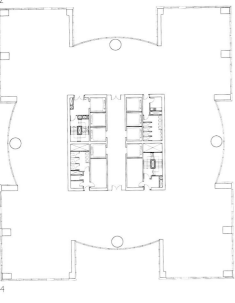

4

1 External view
2 Night view
3 Atrium
4 Typical floor plan
5 Site plan
Photography: courtesy Simon Kwan & Associates Ltd

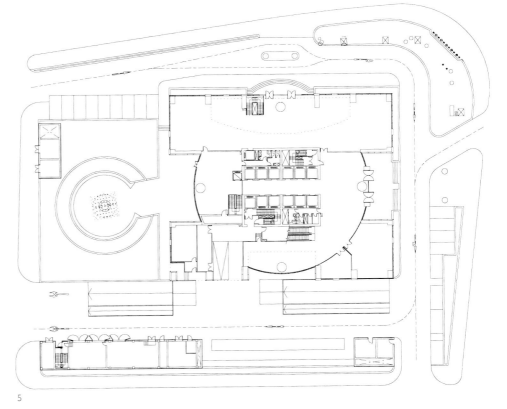

5

Citibank Plaza

■ Known better by its lot number 8888, the site for Citibank Plaza was the last major piece of virgin urban land in Central, Hong Kong, and presented significant design challenges as well as opportunities. On the one hand, it bestrides both the old (Queen's Road Central) and the new commercial core (Admiralty and Queensway), as well as the immediate mid-levels (Peak Tram Station/Government Central Offices) and the waterfront, offering opportunities for linkage and continuity. On the other, it stands adjacent to Hong Kong's newest and most aggressive landmark, the Bank of China, and calls for an appropriate response.

The solution is a twin-tower development with an asymmetrical configuration, rising to 50 and 40 stories and forming an L-shape that embraces an open plaza in front. The plaza is in two interlinked levels relating to the topography of the site, and with walkways and footbridges discharging into it from various strategic destinations it actually functions as a pedestrian traffic node for the neighborhood. While the towers are aligned with the urban axes of the old Central, that is, St John's Cathedral and the Hilton Hotel, the plaza is rotated to respond to the axes of Queensway and the Bank of China, emphasizing the visual continuity of the open space all the way down to Chater Garden.

The asymmetrical massing of the twin towers is a tacit acknowledgment and respect for the step-back profile of the Bank of China, and the selected external finishes of silver/gray mirrored glass, natural aluminum cladding, and flamed granite base ensure a visual compatibility in surface texture and color. But the expression of the new towers complements their neighbor through deliberate contrast, rather than comformity, and in so doing projects its own identity and character. Instead of sharpness and angularity, it portrays curves and rounded corners; instead of a rigid geometric discipline, it emphasizes spontaneous expressions. Aesthetically it reads as a 'constructive synthesis', a collage and juxtaposition of parts that are apparently unstable and incomplete by themselves, but which interact together to compose a dynamic whole—a visual metaphor of the spontaneity and energy of the city's spirit itself.

1

2

Location
Hong Kong SAR, People's Republic of China

Completion
1992

Height
199 m

Stories
47

Area
Site: 8,546 m²; floor: 153,828 m²

Structure
Reinforced concrete

Materials
Exterior: glass and aluminum curtain wall; interior: granite floor and wall, aluminum-panel wall and ceiling

Use
Commercial

Cost
HK$1,800 million

Architect
Rocco Design Ltd

Consultant to Citicorp
Leo A Daly

Structural engineer
Ove Arup & Partners

E/M consultant
J Roger Preston & Partners

Client
Shine Hill Development Ltd

Contractor
Sun Fook Kong Construction Ltd

3

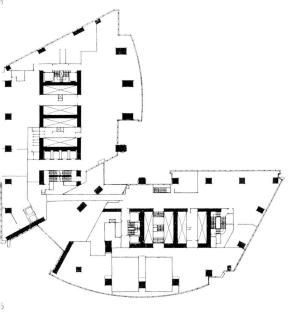

5

Photography: courtesy Rocco Design Ltd and ART Commercial
Workshop

6

Citic Plaza

(Formerly Sky Central Plaza)

■ As the tallest reinforced concrete building structure in the world, Citic Plaza has become the focus of the new business district of Tien Ho and was the talk of the town in Guangzhou when it was completed in 1996. The development consists of two service apartment blocks and an 80-story central office tower, culminating at 390 meters at the summit of the two masts. Widely recognized as the most prominent landmark in Guangzhou and South China, the towers align themselves comfortably on the axis linking the Tien Ho Railway Station to the north and the eminent Tien Ho Stadium to the south. The architecture emphasizes extreme functionalism with the use of modern materials and high technology, pronouncing a distinguished and audacious image, yet one that is strong in appearance. The juxtaposition of square and circular geometry throughout creates a pure, modernized, and everlasting image in a distilled atmosphere.

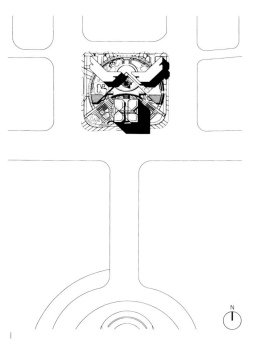

1

2

Location
Guangzhou, People's Republic of China

Completion
1996

Height
Office tower: 390 m (to top of tower mast); 322 m (to top of roof); apartment towers: 142 m

Stories
Office tower: 80; apartment towers: 38

Area
Site: 23,239 m²; office tower: 133,023 m²; apartment towers: 68,819 m²; commercial: 35,073 m²

Structure
Reinforced concrete

Use
Commercial (offices and service apartments)

Cost
US$285.9 million

Architect
Dennis Lau & Ng Chun Man Architects & Engineers (HK) Ltd

Structural engineer
Maunsell Consultants Asia Ltd

Electrical and mechanical engineer
Associated Consulting Engineers`

Main contractor
Kumagai Gammon Joint Venture

Developer
Kumagai SMC Development (Guangzhou) Ltd

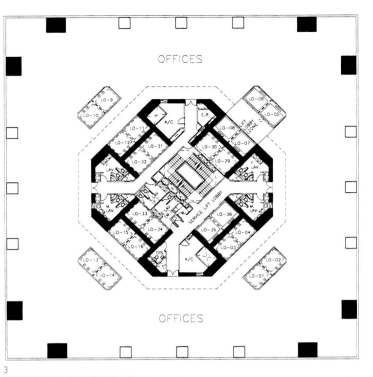

3

4

5

6

1   Site plan
2   View from Tien Ho Stadium
3   Typical floor plan (office tower)
4   Typical floor plan (service apartment T-2)
5   Service apartment entrance
6   Office ground floor lobby
7   Entrance to office tower from Tien Ho North Road
Photography: Frankie Wong & Michael Tse Photography

Conrad International Centennial Singapore

■ The Singapore site for this 35-story hotel posed a number of challenges because of its orientation and irregular shape. In siting the project, it was very important to consider the geometry of the surroundings as well as the irregularities of the site. The hotel tower is therefore oriented respecting the city grid and maximizing the views. The base of the tower is a podium that contains large-scale rooms for a hotel of this type; including a spacious lobby, ballroom, three restaurants, meeting rooms, and service areas. The tower contains 550 hotel rooms and suites. An outdoor pool and restaurant/bar are located on the top of the four-story podium.

The podium is clad in granite and a large glazed canopy creates a generous entrance into the three-story high lobby space. The tower is comprised of a combination of recessed punched windows that form a pattern which is interrupted by a curtain wall skin, which has gentle folds projecting out at several points around the tower.

The hotel is connected to the 46,450 square meter Millenia Mall, which contains high-end retail, restaurants, and theaters. The mall is made up of a series of rhombus-shaped spaces, each topped by a skylight leading to a Great Hall, which opens out into the plaza.

John Sydness was the design partner at John Burgee Architects for this project.

1

Location
Singapore, Republic of Singapore

Completion
1996

Height
109 m

Stories
35

Area
Building: 42,362 m²

Structure
Poured-in-place concrete

Materials
Glass, granite, aluminium

Use
Hospitality

Cost
US$68.5 million

Architect
John Burgee Architects

Associate architect
DP Architects PTE

Structural engineer
Leslie E. Robertson Associates

Service Engineer
Cosentini Associates

Client
Pontiac Marina Pte Ltd Singapore

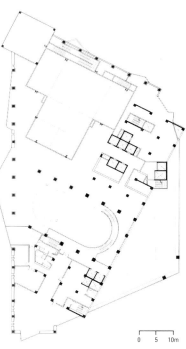

1&2   Southwest view of hotel
3   Main lobby
4   Second floor plan
5   Northwest view of hotel
6   First floor plan
Photography: courtesy Sydness Architect, P. C.

6

The CEC Headquarters Building

■ The CEC Headquarters Building is located on a corner site in downtown Taipei. It is the new home for the oldest and most well-known construction company in Taiwan, the Continental Engineering Corporation.

The building has architecturally finished concrete columns, painted steel bracing, and gray-tinted glass. The form is composed of a square glass box, a back core, and eight massive exterior concrete columns with corner steel bracing. The typical office floor, lit by indirect lighting, is a 25 meter by 25 meter column-free space providing flexible use for the clients. This glass volume also lights up at night exposing the interior spaces and creating an image similar to a film negative.

The main lobby is located on the second floor, lifted off the ground by the huge columns; it is detached from the noise and chaos of the city streets. Special lighting is designed in the massive concrete waffle ceiling in the lobby.

The basement and the lower portion of the building is made of reinforced concrete, the middle part is made of steel reinforced concrete columns and steel truss beams, and the top floor is hung by the roof beams from the top. The top floor is a double-height space with clerestory, which houses the boardroom.

The exoskeleton scheme and the pour-in-place architectural concrete proposed by the architect are great challenges both in design and the construction. Nevertheless, with fine collaboration between the client and the contractor, it has resulted in a powerful yet elegant building.

1

Location
Taipei, Taiwan

Completion
February 1999

Height
49.95 m

Stories
13 and 4 basements

Area
Site: 2,114.75 m²; floor: 17,572.18 m²

Structure
Structural steel

Materials
Architectural concrete, painted steel, aluminum panel, granite, gray-tinted insulating glass unit

Use
Offices

Cost
US$29 million

Architect
Kris Yao/Artech Architects

Structural engineer
Ove Arup & Partners California; Continental Engineering Corp.; Supertech Consultants International

M/E/P engineer
Lincolne Scott Pty Ltd; Continental Engineering Consultants, Inc.

Client
Han Der Construction Co. Ltd

Contractor
Continental Engineering Corp (CEC)

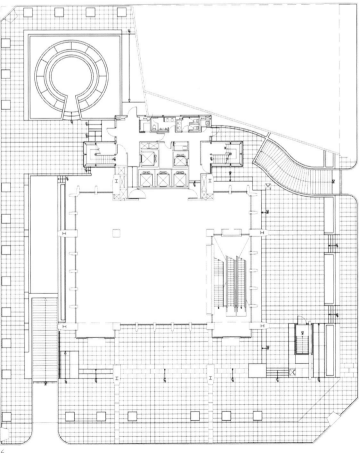

1   Night view
2   Ground floor entrance
3   Main lobby space
4   Interior painted steel stair
5   Exoskeleton details
6   Ground floor plan
Photography: Chyuan-Jen Chang, Jeffery Cheng

Dowa Fire and Marine Phoenix Tower

■ The Dowa Fire and Marine Insurance Co. Ltd headquarters building was constructed as the corporate fiftieth anniversary memorial project. The old Dowa Building at Ume-Shin at the same location had been known and liked by citizens for nearly 60 years. Thus the reconstruction was based on an idea to sustain the characteristics of this landmark for future years. The new building is a complex building consisting of not only functions for the headquarters but also commercial and cultural facilities. These include a concert hall with capacity for 300, a beer hall, a sky restaurant, and a gallery.

1

Location
Osaka, Japan

Completion
October 1995

Height
145.45 m

Stories
29 and 3 basements

Area
Site: 2,324.91 m²; building: 1,258.56 m²;
floor: 30,369.99 m²

Structure
Steel encased in reinforced concrete, and steel frame and reinforced concrete

Materials
Ribbed extruded aluminum, granite

Use
Headquarters building

Architect
Nikken Sekkei Ltd

Client
The Dowa Fire and Marine Insurance Co. Ltd

1   Entire exterior view
2   Frontal view looking up
3   Evening view of entrance
4   Site plan and first floor plan
5   The Phoenix Hall
Photography: Seigan Kuroda (1, 2, 5), SS Osaka (3)

2

3

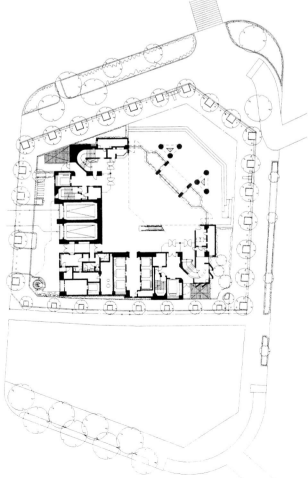

4

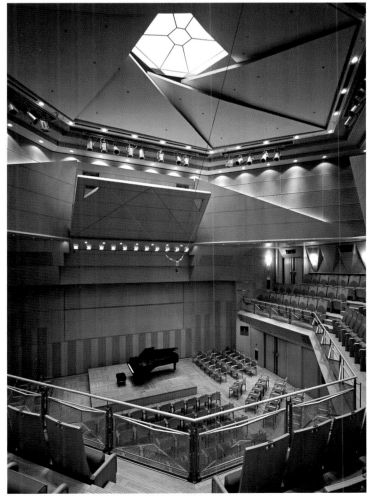

5

Entertainment Building

■ The redevelopment of the Entertainment Building site in Central added a new prestige development to Hong Kong's business district. The site is bound by three streets: Wyndham Street, Wellington Street, and fronts on to Queen's Road Central, Hong Kong's busiest intersection.

The development comprises a one-story basement, a podium, and an office tower above. A multi-level, high-quality retail concourse is formed in the lower levels of the podium. Provision to add bridges in due course, across Wyndham Street and Wellington Street, has also been incorporated. A two-story octagonal 'rotunda' is the focal point of the public courses. Restaurants are formed on the upper podium levels, accessed via escalators and stairs from the public concourse. The lobby adjoins this 'rotunda'.

The square office tower features an articulated back core arrangement, to optimise outlook and to provide the necessary flexibility to the layout of all podium levels. Twenty-six column-free office floors provide a total of 20,000 square meters of first-class office accommodation.

The project features a distinct architectural language, derived from the classical but modified to suit the specific requirements and the Zeitgeist.

Beige-colored granite from Brazil, complemented with silver-gray glass and a matching tin/lead roof define the exterior of the project. White and gray stone paving and timber work are used throughout the interior public areas.

1

2

Location
Hong Kong SAR, People's Republic of China

Completion
August 1993

Height
172 m

Stories
33 and 1 basement

Area
Site: 1,165 m²; superstructure: 20,000 m²

Structure
Reinforced concrete

Materials
Exterior: Brazilian granite, tinted glass, anodized and bronze windows; interior: Brazilian granite, Cardoso and Statuario marble

Use
Commercial

Cost
HK$360 million

Architect
P&T Group

Structural engineer
P&T Group

Service engineer (M&E)
P&T (M&E) Ltd

Client
Chinese Estates Holdings Ltd

Contractor
Paul Y. Construction Co., Ltd

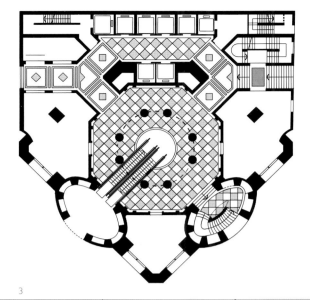

3

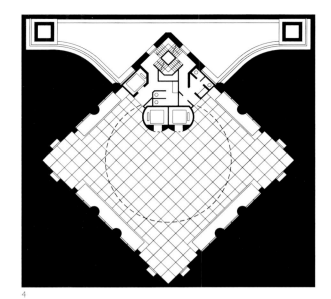

4

5

1   Top of tower
2   View from Queen's Road Central
3   Lobby floor plan
4   Penthouse floor plan
5   Entrance 'Rotunda'
Photography: courtesy P&T Group

Evergreen View Tower

■ Evergreen View Tower is a residential building located in a suburb of Bangkok. The design concerns were creativity, use of space, and the creation of a building identity. Thus, the building is an oval shape with much space around it; this also enables every room to have a view. The building is prominent and interesting, and is in harmony with its surroundings.

1

2

Location
Bangkok, Thailand

Completion
October 1993

Height
121 m

Stories
33

Area
50,000 m²

Structure
Cast-in-place concrete

Materials
Exterior: concrete, aluminum-frame windows

Use
Retail and residential

Cost
400 million Baht

Architect
Plan Architect Co., Ltd; Plan Associates Co., Ltd; Plan Studio Co., Ltd

Structural engineer
Asian Consultant and Technology Co., Ltd

System engineer
Fusion Co., Ltd

Construction management
Plan Consultants Co., Ltd

Client
P. Real Estate Co., Ltd

Contractor
Sang Fah Construction Co., Ltd

3

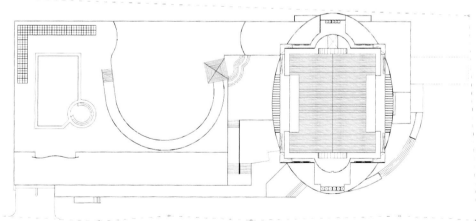

4

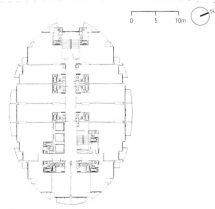

5

6

1 Interior of residential unit
2 Floor elevation
3 View from north
4 Layout plan
5 Typical residential floor plan
6 Elevation
Photography: Evergreen Ville Co., Ltd

Exchange Square I, II, and III

■ The Exchange Square complex consists of two 52-story office towers and a 32-story tower, located in the central business district of Hong Kong on the harbor edge. A public plaza with major sculptures, landscaping, and several water features links the three towers at pedestrian level.

A basement provides carparking and goods' handling facilities, and extends over the whole site.

The design utilizes a rich geometrical order of square and circular elements to achieve a distinct sculptural profile to all towers. A stepped top floor configuration creates attractive penthouses with private terraces, and the American Club on the top floors of Exchange Square II enjoys these facilities.

The structural concept for the towers utilizes an 'outrigger' system in which the widely spaced columns are tied back to the core at the low and mid levels of the towers.

Alternative bands of silver reflective glass and polished pink Spanish granite in modular cladding units provide an attractive and taut enclosure, reinforcing the sculptural qualities of the design.

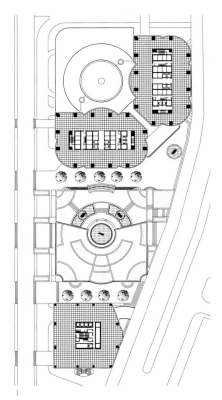

1

2

Location
Hong Kong SAR, People's Republic of China

Completion
1985/1988

Height
192.5 m and 168 m

Stories
Towers I and II: 51 and 1 basement;
Tower III: 30 and 1 basement

Area
Site: 13,400 m²; superstructure: 130,680 m²

Structure
Reinforced concrete

Materials
Exterior: Spanish granite, silver reflective glass, and mirror S.S. accents; interior: Dakota mahogany granite

Use
Hong Kong Stock Exchange and commercial

Cost
HK$2,000 million

Architect
P&T Group

Structural engineer
Ove Arup & Partners

Service engineer (M&E)
J. Roger Preston & Partners / Lands (M&E) Consultancy

Client
Hongkong Land Co. Ltd

Contractor
Gammon Construction Ltd

3

1   *Site plan*
2   *View from Connaught Road Central*
3   *Towers I and II from the forum*
4   *Tree-lined rotunda*
Photography: courtesy P&T Group

4

5 *Axonometric*
6 *Exterior view from platform*
7 *Night view with sculpture by Henry Moore in front entrance*
Opposite:
  View across the harbor

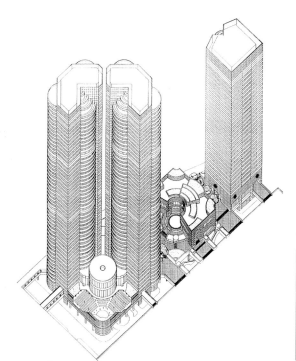

5

6

7

Far East Finance Centre

■ This is a 50-story office development with a total floor area of 48,100 square meters. The tower is designed as a rectangular block with a clean and straightforward elevation treatment. Mechanical and electrical services are concealed behind closely spaced louvers at the refuge floor, and at the roof. The building is finished in gold reflective curtain wall.

The use of a structural steel frame and metal decking shortened the construction time of the superstructure to one year.

1

Location
Hong Kong SAR, People's Republic of China

Completion
1982

Height
180 m

Stories
50

Area
Building: 48,100 m²; site: 3,200 m²

Structure
Structural steel framing

Materials
Interior: granite, marble, and carpet

Use
Commercial

Cost
HK$250 million

Architect
Wong & Ouyang (HK) Ltd

Civil and structural engineer
Wong & Ouyang (Civil-Structural Engineering) Ltd

Electrical and mechanical engineer
Wong & Ouyang (Building Services) Ltd

Client
Green Palm Estates Ltd

Contractor
Right Time Construction Ltd

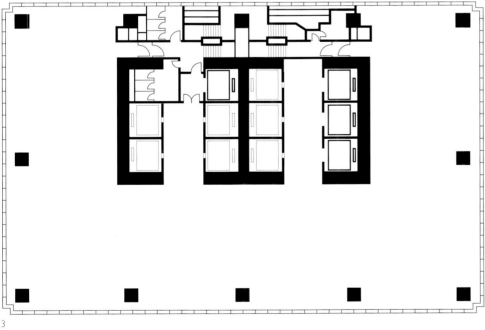

1, 2 & 4   Far East Finance Centre
3   Typical floor plan
Photography: courtesy Wong & Ouyang (HK) Ltd

Fubon Banking Center

■ Fubon Banking Center houses the headquarters of Fubon Corporation. At a total height of 124.6 meters, the building is composed of 24 above-grade floors and six basement floors. The Fubon Banking Retail Center occupies basement floor one and two, while the second floor and above serve as traditional office space. Both functional spaces are accessed from the lobby on the first floor. The transitional division sits on the thirteenth level, where top and bottom spaces are each served by different elevators.

This curtain wall office building, constructed by glass, aluminum, and stone, is located on the heavily treed boulevard, Jen-Ai Road. Service cores of the standard floors are located at the rear of the building, where stone materials are employed in order to contrast the rest of the glass curtain walls façades. The 12.6 meter standard bay of office space and the smaller span found in the rear service cores allow great flexibility of use. The touch-ground window of the south side permits visibility and light.

To echo with the Jen-Ai Road circle a block away in the urban context, a whit wall is curved to the circle's direction and further defines the building form. The vertical staircase is a glass box by day and a vividly illuminated space by night. The building recesses from Jen-Ai Road, creating a plaza that serves as the entrance of the banking center. Five skylight blocks on the plaza bring light into the basement by day and illuminate the pedestrian road by night. Entrance lobby is friendly and welcoming because it is constructed by glass, which breaks the barrier between interior and exterior.

The angled glass box on the top floor serves as the executive floor and the metaphor of an urban billboard of the financial community. Near the glass box are the machine room and the cooling tower, both concealed by a hat-like structure on the rooftop.

1

Location
Taipei, Taiwan

Completion
1995

Height
124.6 m

Stories
24 above-grade, 6 below-grade

Area
Floor: 42,914 m^2

Structure
Steel and reinforced concrete

Materials
Granite, glass curtain wall, aluminum panel

Use
International banking and office facility

Cost
US$80 million

Architect
Skidmore, Owings & Merrill LLP

Joint-venture architect
Kris Yao/Artech Architects

Structural engineer
Evergreen Consulting Engineering Inc.

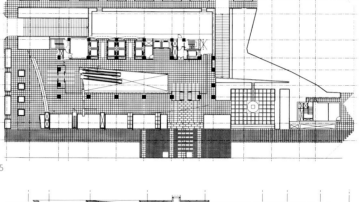

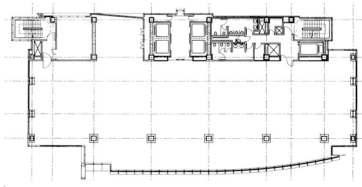

Mechanical engineer
S. Lin Associates, Architects and Engineers

Plumbing/Electrical
Heng Kai Engineering Consultants, Inc.

Client
Chung Hsing Construction Co., Ltd, Fubon Land
Development Co., Ltd

Construction manager
chal Bovis Inc.

1   Night view
2   Ground floor lobby
3   Basement banking center waiting area
4   Front elevation
5   Site plan
6   Typical floor plan
Photography: Wei-Gang Shih, Ray-Tsung Pan

Gateway Plaza

■ The Gateway Office Tower form was developed in response to very stringent planning envelope requirements established for the site, which demanded the building be set on the western edge of the site.

The development comprises 50 levels rising 164 meters above street level with a four-level basement 13 meters below ground. The tower section is diamond-shaped in plan, approximately 70 meters in length, with a maximum in the eastwest direction of 33.5 meters, tapering to 8.5 meters at the north and south extremities, resulting in a height/core width ratio of 17:1.

The high-rise lift shafts are centrally located within the main service core and continue for the full height, while the low-rise and medium-rise extends to level 21 and level 35, respectively. Lower- and medium-rise lift shafts are eccentrically situated with respect to the main core to the western side, ensuring the views to the northeast are not compromised.

The tower floors span approximately 10 meters between the exterior columns and the central service core. To suit the ceiling grid of 1.41 meters, perimeter columns are spaced at 8.4 meter centers. This arrangement allows for greater flexibility in office layout. Maximum natural lighting and views are obtained in the office space due to the high ratio of perimeter window space in relation to floor area.

Four basement areas provide for 210 cars and loading bay facilities for 14 trucks. At levels 5, 6, and 7 an extensive retail centre is provided. A large stepped glazed atrium, framed in structural steel, is located on the eastern side of the tower from levels 5 to 11. The façade of the tower is curtain wall glazing, with expressed mullions and transoms to give the building scale, and framed by structural blades faced with polished Australian granite.

The development also features the restored Paragon Tavern on the corner of Alfred and Loftus Streets, and a new public reserve fronting Loftus Street.

1

Location
Sydney, Australia

Completion
June 1989

Height
165 m above Alfred Street

Stories
46

Area
Site: 5,235 m²

Structure
Concrete-framed building with slip formed concrete service cores

Use
Commercial office

Cost
AUD$165 million

Architect
Peddle Thorp & Walker Pty Ltd

Associate architect
Kann Finch & Partners

Structural engineer
Stigter Clarey & Partners

Mechanical engineer
Norman Disney & Young

Electrical engineer
Lincolne Scott Australia

Client
National Mutual Property Services

Contractor
Concrete Constructions (NSW) Pty Ltd

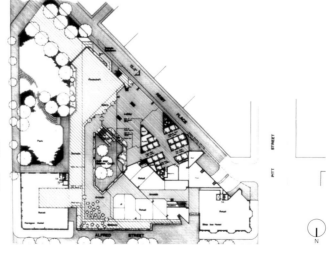

4

1   Glazed atrium over retail concourse
2   Stone-clad entry lobby
3   View to northwest
4   Figured ground plane
Photography: courtesy Peddle Thorp & Walker Pty Ltd

Grand 50 Office Tower

■ Originally intended to be a 20-story office building in Kaohsiung for the Chang Ku group of companies, the design for the Grand 50 was progressively developed to its present height in the late 1980s when developments in the Pacific region made it clear that Taiwanese architects, developers, and construction companies needed to establish their ability to build so-called 'world buildings' in addition to structures of local size.

Inspired by the example of the heavily decorated 1931 Chrysler Building in New York, C. Y. Lee resolved to have the building's architectural design dominate the engineering feat that is always central to such pioneering strutures. In this way, they were able to create what many consider to be the first authentic Chinese skyscraper.

Grand 50 clearly differentiates itself from the glass-clad, steel-frame, geometrical American towers that have, until recently, been the model for super-high buildings all over the world. With the aid of the structural engineer, C. Y. Lee was able to produce a modern, airconditioned, IT-equipped building that successfully combines elements of traditional Chinese architecture with Western technology.

The Grand 50 is a steel-framed, stepped tower, clad from top to bottom in 30 millimeter granite tiles with recessed single windows rather than glass walls. The building's pronounced cantilevered cornice projections and corner set-backs at levels 25, 35, and 45, not only to give it a unique 'battleship' silhouette from a distance, but break up incipient wind vortices that might otherwise become too powerful at street level. The tower itself is capped with a large summit structure that rests on giant consoles. This feature contains an omnidirectional observation deck and restaurant, providing unrivalled views of the city from a height of 222 meters.

Given its relatively small 4,000 square meter site, the Grand 50's total floor area of 83,000 square meters is indicative of the unlimited plot ratios permitted in the port city of Kaohsiung. One of the most remarkable and little-known skyscrapers ever built, the Grand 50 is located on a site some distance from the center of the city in an area scheduled for further private sector redevelopment.

I

Location
Kaohsiung, Taiwan

Completion
1992

Height
222 m

Stories
50 and 5 basements

Area
Site: 4,012 m²; floor: 83,310 m²

Structure
Reinforced concrete and steel

Materials
Exterior: granite

Use
Offices

Cost
$US213 million

Architect
C.Y. Lee & Partners, Architects & Planners

Structural engineer
Evergreen Engineers

Mechanical/Electrical engineer
CEC

Client
Chang Ku Construction Inc.

General contractor
Chang Ku

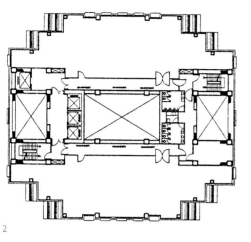

2

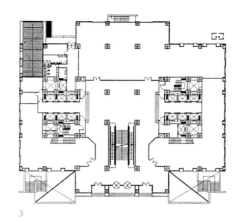

3

4

5

6

7

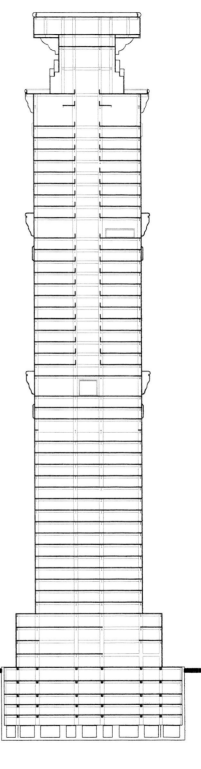

8

1   Night view
2   Fortieth floor plan
3   First floor plan
4   City view
5   Night view
6   Front elevation
7   Elevation detail
8   Transverse section
Photography: courtesy C.Y. Lee & Partners, Architects & Planners

Grand Millennium Plaza/Cosco Tower

■ The project covers an irregular site, previously occupied by severely dilapidated prewar structures, at the western edge of the central business district on Hong Kong Island. As a major urban renewal project, it seeks an urban dialogue with its surroundings. This dialogue is reflected in the modulation of the overall building mass into a High Block and a Low Block that flank a central plaza as a spatial focus for a major pedestrian route among the network of existing narrow passageways.

Within this overall framework, the project attempts to develop a relationship between the old and the new, the historical and the contemporary, influences that are Chinese, and influences that are western.

In an interpretation of traditional Chinese Feng Shui, the High Block (Cosco Tower) with a sturdy base and a pinnacled roof, responding to the hills, was conceived as a 'masculine' element, while the curved Low Block, responding to the sea (historically, the site was right on the waterfront), is the 'feminine' counterpart. The Yin/Yang dichotomy is also reflected in a pointed clock tower in the voluptuous retail podium of the Low Block, and a round lantern feature, the 'drum tower', at the base of the High Block. These features respectively mark the northern and southern entrances to the plaza.

The plaza is built above a future underground railway reserve. The heavy masonry details of the clock and drum towers, arched arcades, metal grilles, fountains, and bronze sculptures are intended to evoke an ambience of the old Hong Kong in this quintessentially historical part of the city. This is juxtaposed by modern elements such as mirror glass curtain walls, embedded neon lighting, exposed escalators, glass canopies, and a large exterior television display screen. As part of this intertwined display of artistry and technology, the plaza also features a sunburst paving pattern with embedded fiber-optic lights that glow in varying colors at night as in a constellation of stars.

I

Location
Hong Kong SAR, People's Republic of China

Completion
March 1998

Height
High Block: 227 m (top of pinnacled roof); Low Block: 123 m (rooftop)

Stories
High Block: 52; Low Block: 29

Area
6,726 m²; High Block: 76,880 m²; Low Block: 36,220 m²

Structure
H-pile foundation and conventional cast in-situ reinforced concrete superstructure ('tube in tube' for High Block)

Materials
Exterior: tinted glass curtain wall with granite claddings and metal grill features at podium levels; interior: stone floor and wall with profiled ceiling (lift lobbies); aluminum and glass shopfront with stone floor and wall features (retail arcade)

Use
High Block: offices; Low Block: offices, retail, government facilities, and public telephone exchange station

Cost
$HK1.7 billion

Architect
Hsin Yieh Architects & Associates Ltd

Structural engineer
Hsin Yieh Architects & Associates Ltd

2

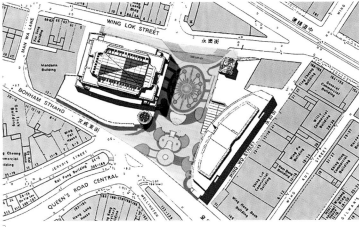

3

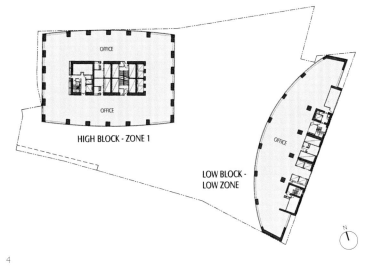

HIGH BLOCK - ZONE 1

LOW BLOCK -
LOW ZONE

4

5

Electrical and mechanical engineer
Associated Consulting Engineers

Quantity surveyor
Levett & Bailey Chartered Quantity Surveyors

Client
Land Development Corporation and New World
Development Co. Ltd

Main contractor
Hip Hing Construction Co. Ltd

1   Cosco Tower with Low Block clock tower
2   Night view from peak
3   Site plan
4   Typical floor plan
5   Upper plaza view
*Photography: courtesy Hsien Yieh Architects & Associates Ltd,
Freeman Wong (1, 3), Alan Chiu (2)*

■ A building of such breadth and height warrants an entrance of consequent scale. Each three of the numerous external columns of the tower were 'gathered' together with V-shaped transfer members into a circular caisson. This changed the ground-floor spacing and height of supports into a suitable larger proportion and gave importance to the circular glazed entrance lobby. Three colorful wall-relief paintings by Frank Stella adorn the gray granite-clad core walls.

The curved façades receive a changing amount of sun radiation at different times. At the east it is the near-horizontal rising sun, at the northeast it is the medium-height morning sun, and at the north it is the high midday sun. A system of external shades has been designed to meet these conditions. They form an integral permanent fixed part of the façade and are planned to intercept the changing sun's rays around the building. Even if not subjected to direct sun, these external shades are beneficial in eliminating glare and avoiding the use of conventional venetian blinds inside.

Considering the superb harbor views available to the building, glass is taken from ceiling to within 30 centimeters of the floor so as to allow a downward angle of view.

Office occupants have often expressed the wish for outdoor terraces to be provided. Responding to this and interspersed over the tower's exterior are 'façade gardens'; deeply recessed, one or more floors high, are planted areas offering relief from the sealed airconditioned environment of typical offices. They are provided for a certain proportion of floors, related to reception areas, boardrooms, and directors' offices, usually near the approaches from elevator lobbies. Their positioning together with the rooftop, north-facing solar collector aperture imparts a deliberate dynamic pattern of shaded interruptions to the otherwise repetitive texture of the façade.

The 14.5 meter clear span of the floors allows freedom of internal planning. On one side of this tenancy are the generously planned executive offices, meeting, and dining rooms, defined by curved glass, solid walls, and polished stone floors. On the other side, workstations and central secretarial desks allow outward views for all occupants. In addition to elevator banks and services, the core contains kitchens, compactus, and security rooms.

Location
Sydney, Australia

Completion
1988

Height
190 m

Stories
44

Area
Net office space: 90,000 m²; floor: 2,000 m²

Structure
Concrete core, steel and concrete floors, granite façades

Materials
Polished granite, tinted glass, aluminum sunshade

Use
Offices

Cost
AUD$190 million

Architect
Harry Seidler & Associates

Associate architect
Dysart & Partners

Structural engineer
Ove Arup

Service engineer
Don Thomas

Client
Superannuation Fund Investment Trust

Contractor
Concrete Constructions

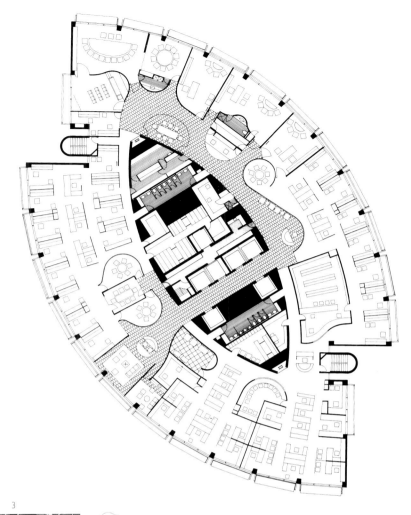

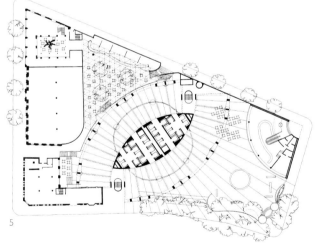

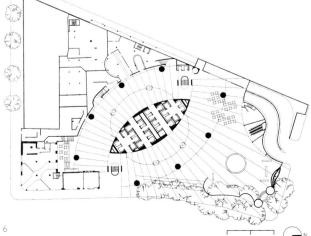

1   North face of tower
2   Ground level view of lobby
3   Typical floor plan
4   Upper plaza food court
5   Upper plaza level plan
6   Lower plaza level plan
Photography: Eric Sierins

2

3

4

5

6

0   10   20m   N

Hang Seng Bank Headquarters Building

■ As the corporate flagship of the Hang Seng Bank, the design of this building reflects the successful business philosophy of the bank, which is to provide customers with a 'smooth and tactful' service. This philosophy is clearly expressed in the treatment of both the interior and exterior of the building.

The tower is clad with aluminum panels at the end walls and with green tinted glass on the front and back, which makes the building highly energy efficient. Adjoining the original headquarters building site, the building rises 27 stories above ground and has three basement floors.

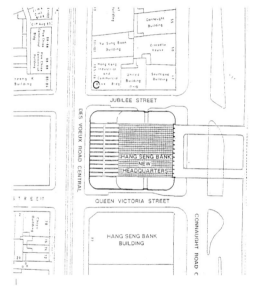

1

2

3

Location
Hong Kong SAR, People's Republic of China

Completion
1989

Height
187.5 m (including basement)

Stories
27 and 3 basements

Area
Building: 35,300 m²; site: 2,100 m²

Structure
Reinforced concrete and structural steel columns

Materials
Exterior: green tinted glass (front and back), aluminum panels (side); interior: granite, curved ceiling panel

Use
Commercial

Cost
HK$1,200 million

Architect
Wong & Ouyang (HK) Ltd

Civil and structural engineer
Wong & Ouyang (Civil-Structural Engineering) Ltd

Electrical and mechanical engineer
BMP Mechanical & Electrical Ltd

External cladding
Heitmann & Associates Inc.

4

5

6

Acoustic
VIPAC Engineers & Scientists Ltd

Lighting
Corbett Design Associates Ltd

Client
Hang Seng Bank Ltd

Contractor
Hip Hing Construction Ltd

1   Site plan
2   Conference room
3   Exterior view
4&5   Banking hall
6   Entrance lobby
Photography: courtesy Wong & Ouyang (HK) Ltd

Head Office of East Japan Railway Company

■ This building is located along the pedestrian network recently provided above the railroad tracks as the future hub of Shinjuku Station's southern exit.

This 28-story skyscraper, rising 150 meters from the ground, is supported by a superstructure that consists of six large, strong built-up columns and a huge built-up beam that spans across three levels. A 20 meter high airwell space is provided at the foot of the superstructure. Another large atrium is provided in the mid-level floors that accommodates cafeterias and reception areas. Several airwells in this high-rise building succeed in creating open and functional spaces.

Curtain walls of clear fleat glass, used for alleviating the indoor reflection of illumination at night and for enhancing the daytime appearance, are curved so that they not only prevent radiowaves jamming, but also give formality to the building.

1

2

Location
Tokyo, Japan

Completion
September 1997

Height
150 m

Stories
28

Area
3,225 m²

Structure
Steel frame and reinforced concrete super-frame

Materials
Ceramic plate, clear fleat glass

Use
Head office

Architect
Nikken Sekkei Ltd

Associate architect
JR East Design Corporation

Client
East Japan Railway Company

Contractor
Kajima Corporation, Tekken Corporation, Taisei Corporation, Odakya Construction Co. Ltd

3

4

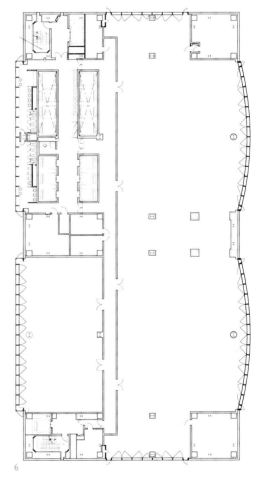

6

5

1   Around the entrance
2   Exterior view from east
3   Central reception area on eighteenth floor
4   Dining hall on fifteenth floor
5   Night view of fourth floor lobby
6   Floor plan (floors 6–14)
Photography: Hiroshi Shinozawa

Hong Kong Convention and Exhibition Centre

■ The Hong Kong Trade Development Council's brief was a 73,000 square meter exhibition center of a world-class standard. It is the nucleus of a hotel/office complex made up of a 575-room deluxe-class hotel (Grand Hyatt Hong Kong); an 868-room tourist-class hotel (Renaissance Harbour View); 670 luxury-class serviced apartments (Convention Plaza Apartments); an office tower of 56,430 square meters; and a 1,070-space public carpark.

The exhibition and conference facilities are comprised of two 11,500 square meter exhibition halls; a convention hall with the capacity to seat 2,700; 150-table Chinese-style banquet area; two auditoria of 300 and 800 seats respectively; and a number of meeting rooms.

2

1

3

Location
Hong Kong SAR, People's Republic of China

Completion
1990

Height
168.80 m

Stories
(Above the convention and exhibition podium)
Grand Hyatt: 23; Renaissance Harbour View Hotel: 30; serviced apartments: 38; office tower: 38

Area
Site: 30,000 m²

Structure
Podium: structural steel; towers: reinforced concrete

Materials
Exterior: natural granite cladding, window wall system and structural glass wall system; interior: natural stone and metal cladding

Use
Exhibition and conference hall, deluxe hotel, office tower, and serviced apartments

Cost
US$461.5 million

Architect
Dennis Lau & Ng Man Architects & Engineers (HK) Ltd (originally known as Ng Chun Man & Associates Architects & Engineers (HK) Ltd)

Structural engineer
Dennis Lau & Ng Man Architects & Engineers (HK) Ltd

Service engineer
Parson Brinckerhoff

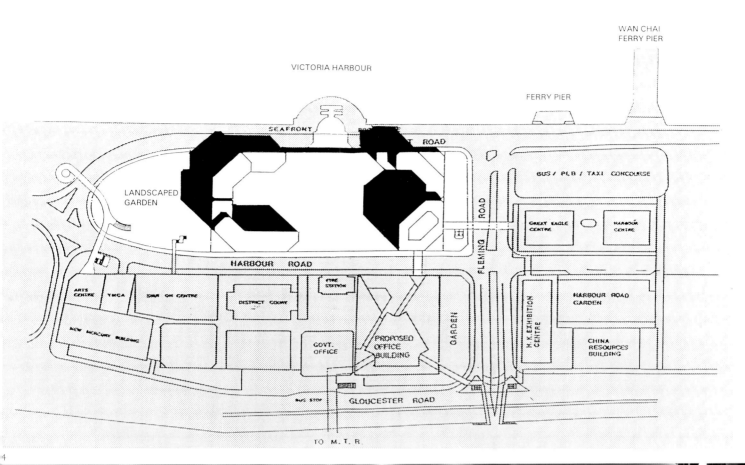

4

5

Interior designer
Hirsch/Bedner & Associates

Client
The Hong Kong Trade Development Council,
New World Development Ltd

Main contractor
Hip Hing Construction Ltd

1   Entrance lobby of Grand Hyatt Hotel
2   View from Victoria Harbour
3   View of vehicular drop-off area at Hong Kong Convention and
    Exhibition Centre
4   Site plan
5   View of auditorium
Photography: Frankie Wong & Michael Tse Photography

Hongkong and Shanghai Banking Corporation Headquarters

■ The bank stands at the head of Statue Square, one of the most spectacular sites in Hong Kong. Conceived during a sensitive period in the former colony's history, the building was a statement of confidence, created without compromise: the brief was for nothing less than 'the best bank building in the world'.

Through a process of questioning and challenging—including the involvement of a feng shui geomancer—the project addressed the nature of banking in Hong Kong and how it should be expressed in built form. In doing so, it virtually reinvented the office tower. The requirement to build in excess of a million square feet, in a short timescale, required a high degree of prefabrication, including factory-finished modules, while the need to build downwards and upwards simultaneously led to the adoption of a suspension structure with pairs of steel masts arranged in three bays. This allowed another radical move—the service cores could be pushed to the perimeter to create flexible, deep-plan floors around a 10-story atrium. The pedestrian plaza created beneath the building has become a lively weekend picnic spot. Escalators rise up from the plaza to the main banking hall with its glass underbelly. A mirrored 'sunscoop' reflects sunlight down through the heart of the building to the plaza floor.

The 'bridges' that span between the masts define double-height reception areas. These spaces break down the scale of the building both visually and socially, creating village-like clusters of space. A unique system of movement through the building combines high-speed lifts to the reception spaces with escalators beyond.

The building form is articulated in a stepped profile of individual towers—respectively 28, 35, and 41 stories high—which create floors of varying width and depth, garden terraces, and distinctive east and west elevations. From the outset the bank placed a high priority on flexibility. Since its completion, it has been able to reconfigure office layouts with ease, even incorporating a large dealers' room into one floor—a move that could not have been anticipated when the building was designed.

I

Location
Hong Kong SAR, People's Republic of China

Completion
1985

Height
183 m

Stories
28, 35 and 41

Area
99,000 m²

Structure
Suspension structure

Materials
Concrete, steel, aluminum, and glass

Use
Bank and offices

Cost
£500 million

Architect
Foster and Partners

Structural engineer
Ove Arup & Partners (HK) Ltd

Client
Hongkong and Shanghai Banking Corporation

Contractor
John Lok/Wimpey Joint Venture

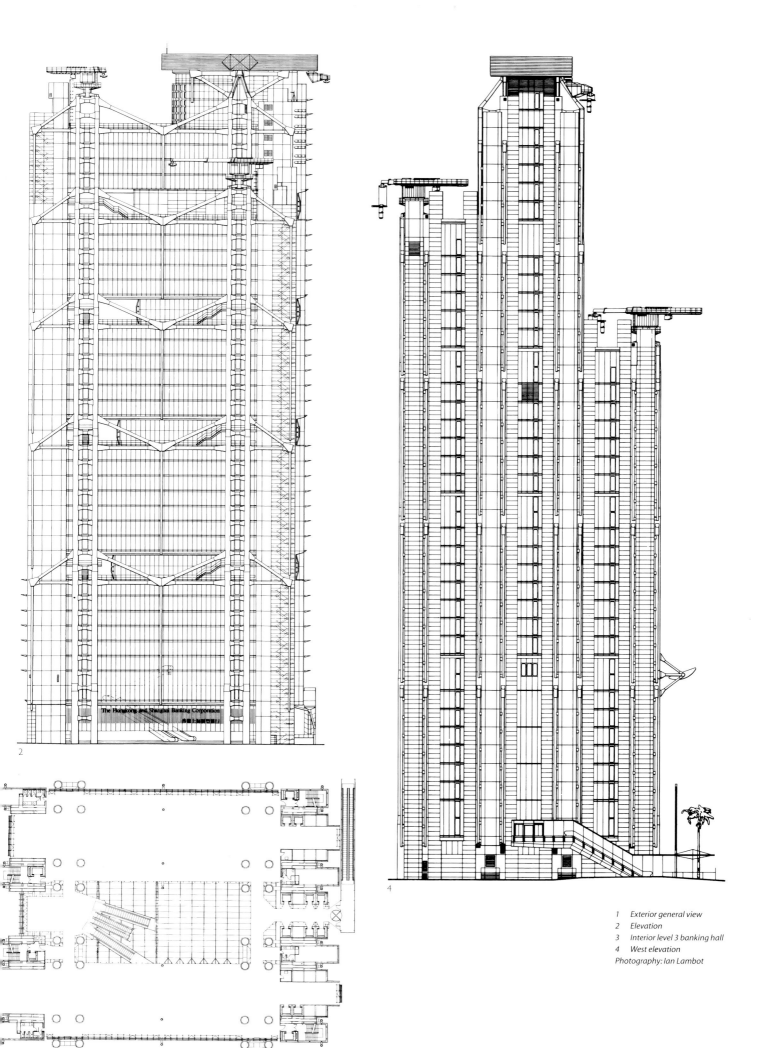

2

4

1   Exterior general view
2   Elevation
3   Interior level 3 banking hall
4   West elevation
Photography: Ian Lambot

Horizon Apartments

■ The 43-story tower is shaped to gain the widest sweep of harbor outlook, centered on Sydney's Opera House and the Harbour Bridge. The rest of the site, excavated to house a five-story, 500-car garage, accommodates on its deck a 25 meter swimming pool and tennis court, which is overlooked from the terraces of surrounding low-rise split-level apartments.

The tower contains two penthouses, 18 three-bedroom apartments (135 square meters), 157 two-bedroom apartments (100 square meters, 105 square meters and 115 square meters), and 54 one-bedroom apartments (55 square meters). The townhouses consists of 22 one-bedroom/studio apartments, eight two-bedroom apartments, and one three-bedroom apartment.

The apartment tower planning divides the floor space evenly between living and bedroom portions, making these interchangeable in plan, which makes possible combinations and side reversal of two-bedroom and three-bedroom apartments.

To maximize the magnificent sweep of views towards the harbor, Opera House, Harbour Bridge, and city skyline, the tower is shaped to reflect the view arc from north to west.

As the views become increasingly dramatic with increased height, taking in the Pacific Ocean as well as Sydney Harbour, the orientation of the balconies changes in the top quarter of the tower, which contains the larger apartments.

To take full advantage of the spectacular views, living and main bedrooms have full glass walls, with narrow horizontal windows to kitchens and second bedrooms. All windows are sun-protected either by the terrace overhangs or special exterior awnings to obviate the need for venetian blinds (which would block the view).

Approximately 20 percent of the site is covered by buildings, with the remainder extensively landscaped, and containing a swimming pool, barbecue area, and tennis court.

1

2

Location
Sydney, Australia

Completion
1997

Height
139 m

Stories
43

Area
32,000 m²

Structure
Prestressed concrete

Materials
Concrete façade

Use
Apartments

Architect
Harry Seidler & Associates

Structural engineer
Bruechle Gilchrist & Evans

Mechanical engineer
Addicoat Hogarth Wilson

Client
Elarosa Investments

Contractor
Grocon

3

5

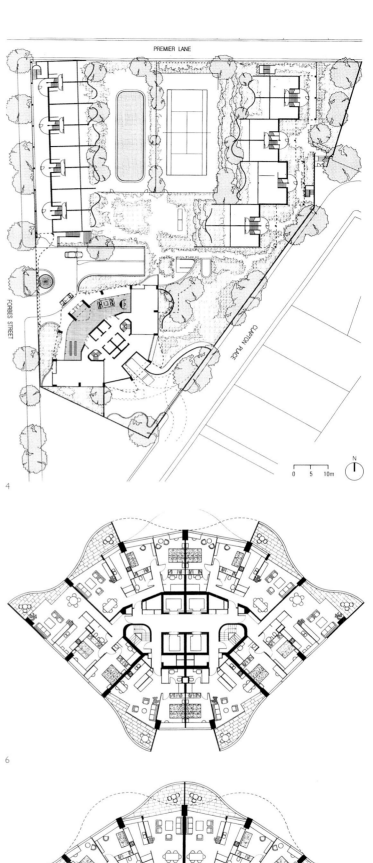

4

6

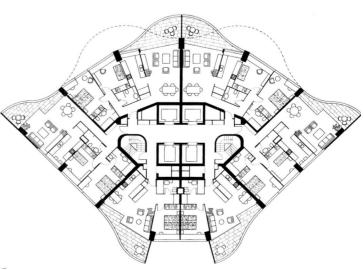

7

1   Apartment interior view
2   View looking up at tower from entry drive
3   View of tower from gardens across swimming pool
4   Site plan
5   View from apartment towards city and harbor
6   Floor plan (levels 7, 9, 11, 13, 15 17, 19, 21, 27, 29)
7   Floor plan (levels 3–6)
Photography: Eric Sierins

ICEC/LKG Tower

■ This 39-story office tower for the International Copra Export Corporation is located on a midblock site on Ayala Avenue in Makati—a major commercial district in greater Manila. The scheme employs ideas found in Philippine architecture and decorative arts, combining them with modern planning strategies and building technology to create a building that is at once international and evocative of place.

The Philippine decorative tradition is a fusion of Malay, Spanish, Chinese, and American influence. It finds expression in a culture of pattern-making, which favors delicate geometric or vegetal forms. Evident in the vernacular application of architectural details, loomed indigenous textiles and embroidery, these patterns frequently lack the reading of an overall figure, identifying fields of lightly contrasted texture and scale instead. In this project, a variety of these patterns have been interpreted in the development of the massing, the exterior wall, and the lobby elevations. The patterns created also define fields, which interact with each other to animate the form of the tower. At the same time, they help make the project a site-specific work by employing a repertory of formal devices familiar to its users.

Mindful of the extremities of a tropical climate, managing sunlight, and maximizing air circulation are key determinants in the design of the tower. The diversity of sun-control and fanning devices found in traditional structures attests to the importance of these considerations in Philippine architecture. Sunscreens and grilles are incorporated in the curtain wall system to supplement airconditioning and tinted glass; various elements that compose the lower volume of the tower project forward to provide shade.

1

Location
Manila, Philippines

Completion
January 2001

Height
180.10 m

Stories
39

Area
46,450 m²

Structure
Concrete frame superstructure, unitized aluminum and reflective glass curtain wall with intergrated sunscreens

Materials
Lobby walls: Paldao wood veneer, Thassos white marble, white gold leaf and front silk-screened laminated glass; floor: honed Verde Mergozzo granite with Ostrich Grey slate; ceiling: white gold leaf and silver painted aluminum

Use
Office tower with three dining levels, a banking hall, parking for 500 cars, an owner's penthouse, and a helipad for VIP access on the roof

Architect
Kohn Pedersen Fox Associates PC

Associate architect
Recio & Casas

Structural engineer
Ove Arup & Partners

Mechanical engineer
Flack & Kurtz, R. J. Carlo & Partners

Client
International Copra Export Corporation Land Company

Contractor
Design Coordinates, Inc.

2

3

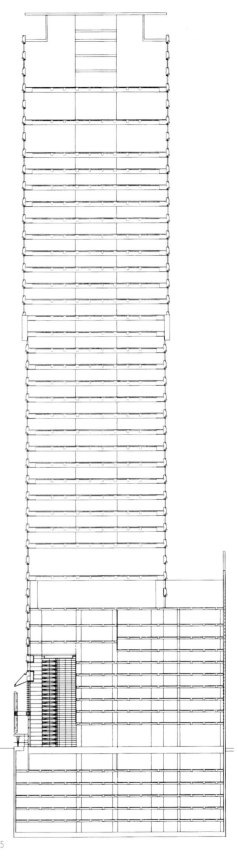

5

4

1   View along Ayala Avenue
2   View of curtain wall
3   Elevator lobby
4   Main building lobby
5   Section looking north

*Photography: courtesy of Kohn Pedersen Fox Associates/
Dicky Herras*

JAIC Hilton Tower

■ The 34-story JAIC Hilton Tower was developed to provide a residential complex for foreign nationals with extended stay assignments in the region. The tower was designed for a total of 175 dwelling units, varying from two-bedroom and three-bedroom units to luxury units at the penthouse level.

Supporting the residential tower is the base or podium element housing public-use spaces. The podium portion was designed with restaurants and shops arranged in a mini-mall atmosphere on the ground floor offering easy access at street level. Floors two through four are for automobile parking. The fifth floor, or the top portion of the podium, is devoted to amenities for the residents such as a roof garden, tennis court, squash court, and athletic club.

The high-rise tower contains the residential units. With few tall buildings to share the views, each residence offers panoramic views from the living and bedroom units of the City of Colombo, the Indian Ocean, and Lake Beira. As enjoyable as these views are for the residents, consideration was given to the community viewing the tower against the skyline. The building's exterior elevation was designed in response to the off-set floor plan as well as designing windows of differing size to articulate a variety of forms in creating the building elevations. Color was applied in gradient tones in an effort to soften the building mass. In addition, part of the program was to honor the request from the neighboring government guesthouse staff to visually safeguard their privacy as well as their security. The solution to this was to close the side wall and utilize the main structural shear wall.

Since the site was originally zoned for light industrial use (a tea company was the previous occupant), the utilities serving the site were not adequate for the new residential and commercial use. However, the project was designated by the government as a 'national flagship status', resulting in prioritized assistance from the local governing authorities and public utility companies in providing the necessary infrastructure requirements.

The property is managed by the Hilton Hotel Company as an extended-stay hotel. Hilton has established a presence in the area having managed a property in downtown Colombo for many years.

1

Location
Colombo, Sri Lanka

Completion
June 1997

Height
116 m (without mast); 129 m (with mast)

Stories
34

Area
46,035 m²

Structure
Reinforced concrete

Materials
Podium wall: granite/texture coating paint; tower wall: texture coating paint

Use
Commercial, residential, serviced apartments

Cost
US$47 million

Architect
Kajima Design Asia Pte Ltd (KDA)

Associate architect
Consortium 168

Structural engineer
KDA / SCE

Service engineer
KDA / Shin Nippon Air Technologies Co., Ltd

Client
Japan Asia Investment Co., Ltd (JAIC)

Contractor
KAJIMA & AOKI Joint Venture

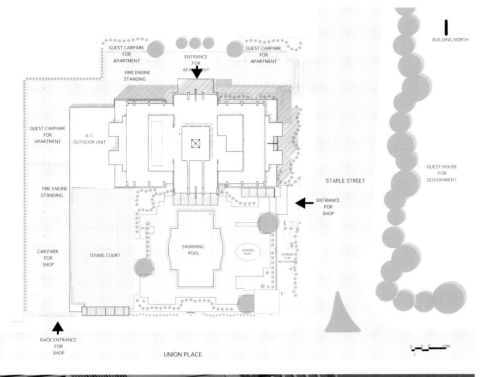

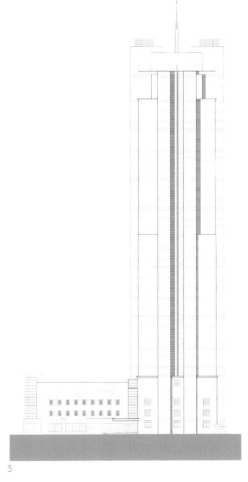

1 Main façade
2 Site plan
3 Roof garden level
4 Podium side wall
5 West-side elevation
Photography: courtesy Kajima Design Asia Pte Ltd (KDA)

Jardine House
(Formerly Connaught Centre)

■ Rising 52 stories above the reclaimed land upon which it was built, Jardine House, formerly known as the Connaught Centre, was for many years the tallest building in Asia.

Located right at the harbor front, the distinctive circular windows are a familiar reminder of the nautical foundation from which Hong Kong's history and economy emerged. A shining metal skin wraps around the external walls forming a concrete shear wall box, eliminating interior columns in the office space. This frame is supported on massive transfer columns at ground level.

The landscaped plaza with water features is punctuated by sculptural elements that lead to the shops below.

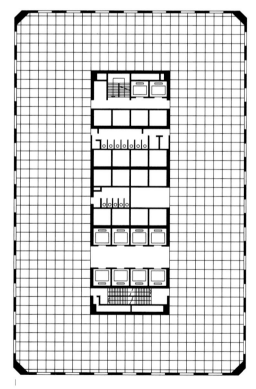

1

2

Location
Hong Kong SAR, People's Republic of China

Completion
1973

Height
178 m

Stories
52 and 2 basements

Area
Superstructure: 90,000 m²; basement: 10,000 m²

Structure
Reinforced concrete

Materials
Exterior: natural anodized aluminum and reflective glass; interior: slate and 'Albi Verde' marble

Use
Commercial

Cost
HK$145 million

Architect
Palmer and Turner

Structural engineer
Mitchell McFarlane & Partners

Service engineer
Lands (M&E) Consultants

Client
Hongkong Land Co. Ltd

Contractor
Gammon Construction Ltd

3

4

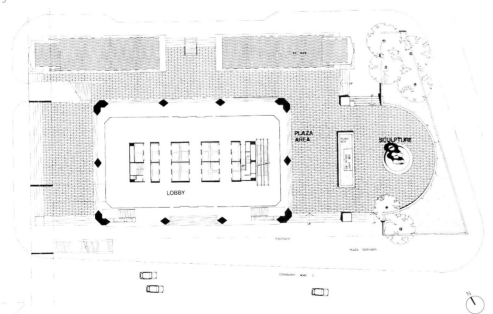

5

1   Floor plan
2   View from Statue Square
3   View of Pilotis
4   View from Victoria Harbour
5   Site plan
Photography: courtesy P&T Group

Jin Mao Tower

■ Located in the Pudong District of the city's Lujiazui Finance and Trade Zone in Shanghai, the Jin Mao Tower is a 278,800 square meter multi-use development incorporating office, hotel, retail, service amenities, and parking. The 88-story tower houses hotel and office space, with a 555-room Grand Hyatt Hotel in the top 38 stories affording impressive views of the city and the surrounding region. Office spaces in the lower 50 stories are easily accessed. Jin Mao's six-story podium houses hotel function areas, a conference and exhibition center, a cinema auditorium, and a 21,000 square meter retail galleria. The base of the tower is surrounded by a landscaped courtyard with a reflecting pool and seating, offering visitors a peaceful retreat from Shanghai's busy street activity.

In addition to the tower and podium, Jin Mao incorporates three below-grade levels with a total area of 57,000 square meters. These levels accommodate parking for 993 cars and 1,000 bicycles; hotel service facilities; additional retail space; a food court; an observatory elevator lobby; and building systems equipment areas including electrical transformers and switchgear, a sewage treatment plant, a domestic water plant, a boiler room, and a chiller plant.

The building systems design integrates intelligent building features that provide life safety, security, and comfort; high levels of energy efficiency; ease of building maintenance, operation, and control; and technologically advanced communications systems. Advanced structural engineering concepts employed in the design of the tower protect it from the typhoon winds and earthquakes typical of the area.

The tower recalls historic Chinese pagoda forms, with setbacks that create a rhythmic pattern. Its metal and glass curtain wall reflects the constantly changing skies, while at night the tower shaft and crown are illuminated. At 420.5 meters, the tower and its spire are a significant addition to the Shanghai skyline. Jin Mao's completion makes it the tallest building in China and the centerpiece of Shanghai.

1

Location
Shanghai, People's Republic of China

Completion
April 1999

Height
420.5 m (street level to top of spire)

Stories
88

Area
278,800 m²

Materials
Reinforced concrete, structural steel, stainless steel, granite, high-performance glass, aluminum

Use
Multi-use complex housing office, hotel, retail, and parking components

Cost
US$540 million

Architect
Skidmore, Owings & Merrill LLP

Associate architect
East China Architectural Design and Research Institute (construction phase); Shanghai Institute of Architectural Design and Research (pre-construction phase)

Structural engineer
Skidmore, Owings & Merrill LLP

Service engineer
Skidmore, Owings & Merrill LLP (MEP)

Client
China Shanghai Foreign Trade Centre Company, Ltd

Contractor
Shanghai Jin Mao Contractor

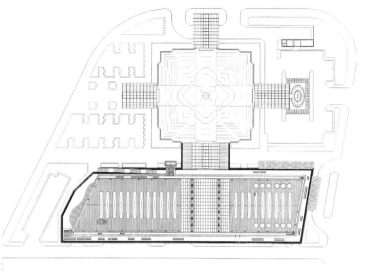

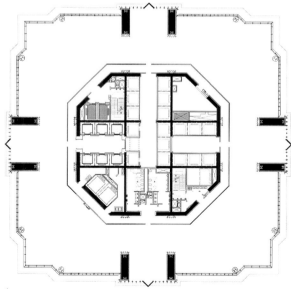

1   Elevation
2   Site plan
3   Grand Hyatt hotel entry
4   Grand Hyatt hotel atrium
5   Podium interior
6   Typical floor plan
Photography: Hedrich Blessing, Nick Merrick

JR Central Towers and Station

■ The Japan Railway Central Towers is a project situated in the western part of Nagoya, a city midway between Tokyo and Osaka. Adjacent to the tracks of the Shinkansen, the national high-speed trains that connect the city to the rest of Japan, the complex houses cultural, hotel, office, and station facilities. The design solution addresses the unique structural problem of creating a complex, mixed-use building on top of an important transportation hub, linking rail, subway, and bus lines along a densely populated urban corridor. Organizing the large flow of people associated with a variety of use types, the solution defines distinct and separate circulation paths for pedestrians using different aspects of the building.

The project is composed of two towers rising from a 20-story podium. The base contains a multilevel department store, museum, health club, multipurpose hall, restaurants, and other retail functions. A two-story 'skystreet' on the fifteenth floor—accessed from the ground level through a bank of exterior shuttle elevators—connects public functions below to the towers above as it affords sweeping views of the city. The circular 59-story hotel tower provides a variety of room types and views; the 55-story office tower is formed by the juxtaposition of cylindrical and rectilinear forms.

The contrast between the towers and their shared base also reflects the desire to integrate the building into the urban context at different levels. Evoking parallel stretches of rail, the horizontal articulation of the podium provides a link to the low, surrounding context. The uninterrupted vertical expression of the towers, combined with the siting of the complex, forms a monumental gateway into the city, confirming the building's role as a locus for future high-rise developments.

1

Location
Nagoya, Japan

Completion
2000

Height
Hotel: 245 m; office: 226 m

Stories
Hotel: 59; office: 55

Area
Floor: 445,920 m²

Materials
Pre-cast concrete curtain wall panels with glass and ceramic tiles; glass and aluminum curtain wall; aluminum panel cladding

Use
Mixed-use facility

Architectural design consultant
Kohn Pedersen Fox Associates PC

Architectural design team
Taisei Corporation; Sakakura Associates; JR Tokai

Associate architect
Taisei Corporation

Structural engineer
Taisei Corporation

Service engineer
Taisei Corporation

Client
JR Tokai

Contractor
Lead contractor of the Joint Venture Construction Team: Taisei Corporation

3

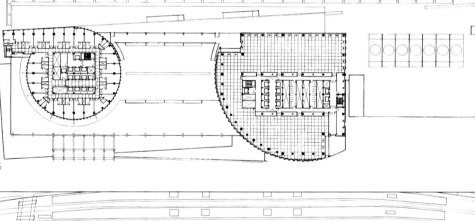

5

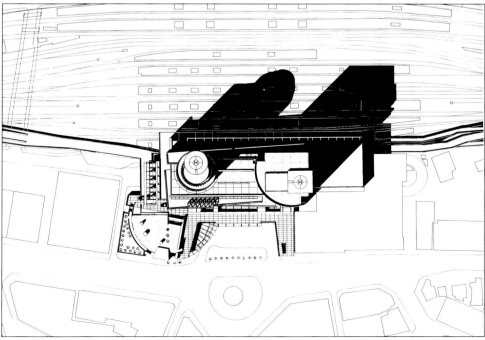

View from east at street level
Fifteenth floor shuttle elevator lobby at 'skystreet'
Fifteenth floor 'skystreet' looking north
View from west from train tracks
Typical tower plans
Site plan
Photography: courtesy Kohn Pedersen Fox Associates PC

K. Wah Centre

■ The concept for this prominent 28-story office tower on the North Point waterfront derives from a Neolithic jade sculpture, a 'cong', in which the interpenetrating of cylindrical and rectangular volumes represents the conjoining of heaven and earth. The outcome is an ideal synergy of inspiration and design; the form of the artifact and the functionality of the central service core and open layout combination are mutually reinforcing.

At the urban scale, consistent treatment of the building surface objectifies the building and creates a unified impression.

Selective openings in the cylindrical and rectangular forms accommodate balconies, reveal the composite volume, and allow the column structure to become expressed at the building corners.

Reflective, green-tinted glass is utilized in the curtain wall design to diminish glare and to channel the interplay of light between sea and sky.

The waterfront location and efficient floor layout ensure inspiring, panoramic views of Victoria Harbour and the entire Hong Kong metropolis.

1

Location
Hong Kong SAR, People's Republic of China

Completion
1991

Height
92.35 m

Stories
28

Area
Site: 1,858 m²; floor: 27,958 m²

Structure
Reinforced concrete/beam and column

Materials
Exterior: glass curtain wall, granite finish; interior: marble (lobby)

Use
Offices

Cost
HK$200 million

Architect
Simon Kwan & Associates Ltd

Structural engineer
MMBP International Ltd

Services engineer
Lu & Associates

Client
K. Wah Group

Contractor
Hoi Ning Engineering Co. Ltd

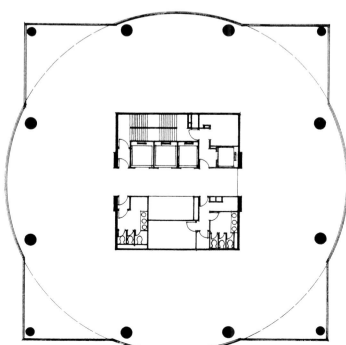

1 External view
2 Lift lobby
3 Typical floor plan
Photography: courtesy Simon Kwan & Associates Ltd

Keyence Corporation Headquarters Building

■ Sleek lines and a marked lack of artifice are the hallmarks of the Keyence Shin-Osaka Building in central Osaka. Home base to a manufacturer of advanced factory automation, the structure epitomizes simplicity at every turn.

The framework comprises 25 x 25 meter square grids of exposed steel with pairs of cross beams supported by sets of double pillars, constructed around a 3 meter external core.

Windows on all four sides allow each floor to be divided into several smaller zones as needed, without compromising the plentiful supply of natural light that enters the interior space. The multi-layered glazing on the windows helps reduce heating and cooling requirements year-round.

1

2

Location
Osaka, Japan

Completion
July 1994

Height
101 m

Stories
21 and 1 underground

Area
Building: 21,633 m²

Structure
Steel, reinforced concrete, and steel-framed reinforced concrete

Use
Offices

Architect
Nikken Sekkei Ltd

Client
Keyence Corporation

Contractor
Obayashi Corp.

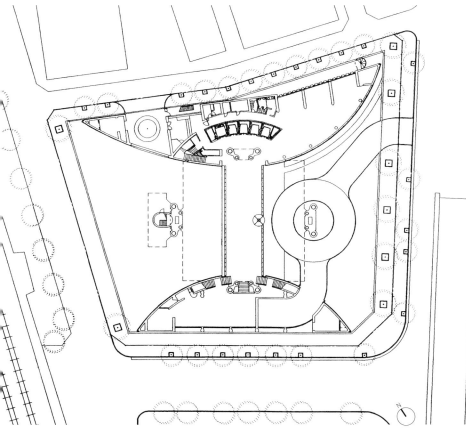

5

1 Elevation
2 Exterior view
3 Around the entrance
4 Site plan
5 Entrance hall
Photography: S.S. Osaka (2,5); Minotu Karamatsu (1,3)

King Tower

■ This tower is the headquarters of the Jin Qiao Reprocessing Zone in the new development area of Shanghai. The building is divided vertically into two zones: the upper zone houses the headquarters while the lower zones are for tenants.

Elevators rise to a lobby area about mid-way up the building, which is visible as a recess on the elevation. From there, a second set of elevators provide access to the headquarters.

The exterior incorporates a blue-tinted glass canopy, five stories in height, that sweeps down and out to cover the main entrance.

The steel girders continue above the roof to form a 15 meter pinnacle.

The design endeavors to create a visual symbol to capture the dynamic spirit of the high-tech industrial development of the new Shanghai.

1

2

Location
Shanghai, People's Republic of China

Completion
1996

Height
208 m

Stories
38

Area
Site: 16,504 m²; floor: 52,000 m²

Structure
Steel, thermal double-glazing curtain wall

Use
Offices, headquarters of the Jin Qiao Export Processing Zone

Architect
Taoho Design Architects Ltd

Structural engineer
East China Architectural Design Institute Shanghai

Client
Jin Qiao Export Processing Zone

Contractor
First Company of China State Construction Third Bureau

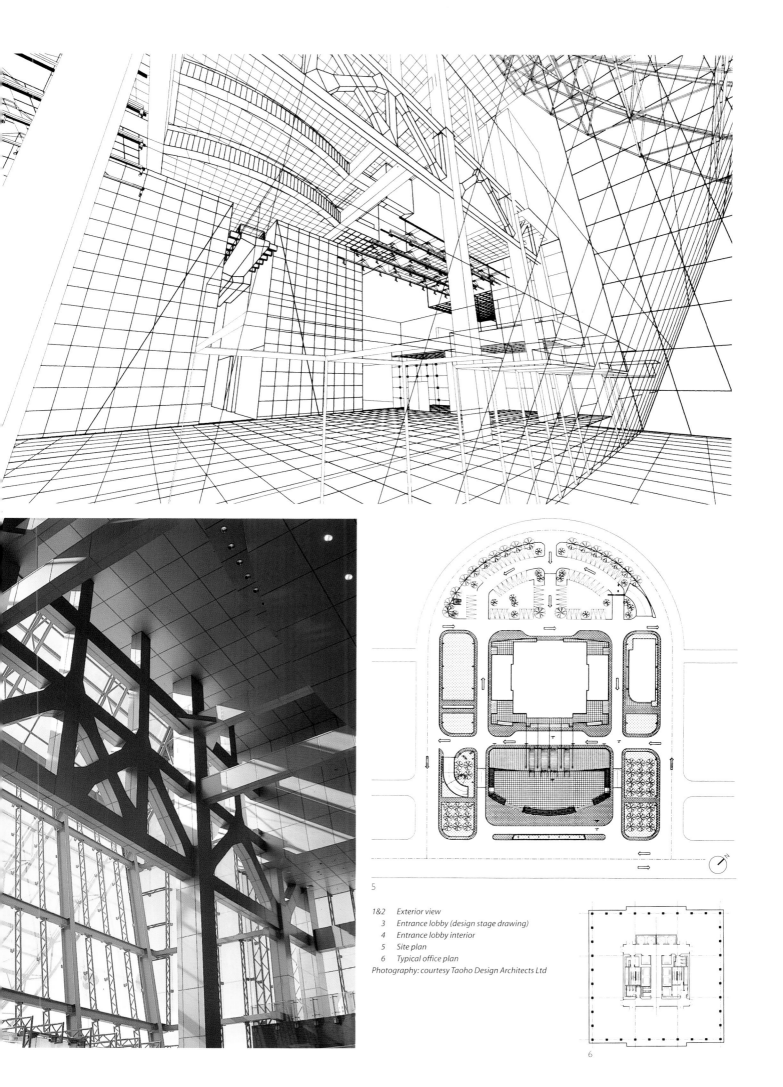

5

1&2 Exterior view
  3 Entrance lobby (design stage drawing)
  4 Entrance lobby interior
  5 Site plan
  6 Typical office plan
Photography: courtesy Taoho Design Architects Ltd

6

Landmark Tower

■ Synthesizing oriental sensibility with contemporary technology, the elegantly tapered Landmark Tower is the focal point of Minato Mirai 21 at the portal harborfront of Yokohama, Japan. Developed as the first phase of a 427,130 square meter megastructure, the 73-story, 296 meter high skyscraper is the tallest building in Japan.

Bounded by the elevated moving sidewalks from Sakuragi-cho Station at the southern corner and from the Grand Mall at the northeast, the 38,000 square meter Block 25 site is the symbolic and physical gateway to the coastal district being redeveloped by the municipal government.

Combined in form as one distinctive building, the granite-clad tower includes 162,649 square meters of office space on 52 floors and 88,530 square meters of hotel space on 15 floors at the top of the tower. Uppermost hotel floors are projected out to accommodate two restaurants and an observation deck with a panoramic view to Tokyo Bay, Mount Fuji, and Tokyo. A skylit swimming pool and health facilities are located at the base of the hotel portion where it is recessed over the office floors. Other hotel facilities such as lobby, banquet, and reception rooms occupy the lower four floors in the southwest part of the retail block. Accommodating the need for a large vertical core, especially in the lower portions, the steel and concrete structure starts with a wide star-shaped base and slopes upward, becoming progressively slender.

At the third retail level, a skylighted vertical circulation point marks the connection of the moving sidewalk to the main pedestrian mall integrating the complex. Extending northeast, the spine is lined by four levels of shops and restaurants and culminates in a dramatically enclosed atrium space. Three levels of service and parking below ground accommodate a total of 1,400 cars.

1

Location
Yokohama, Japan

Completion
July 1993

Height
296 m

Stories
73 (with penthouse) and 3 below ground

Area
Project: 427,130 m²; site: 38,061.51 m²

Cost
US$1 billion, ¥270 billion

Architect
The Stubbins Associates

Schematic design/Design development/Construction documents/Site supervision
Mitsubishi Estate Architectural and Engineering Office

Structural engineer
LeMessurier Consultants Inc.

Mechanical/Electrical engineer
Syska & Hennessy

Client
Mitsubishi Estate Company Limited

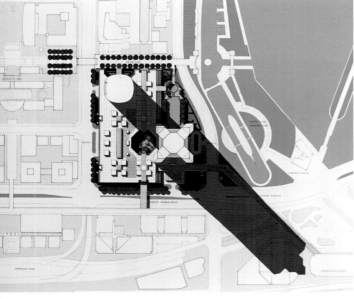

2   Building with Mount Fuji backdrop
3   View from downtown Yokohama
4   Site plan
5   High-rise floor plan (levels 36–52)
6   Building lobby
Photography: courtesy Mitsubishi Estate Company

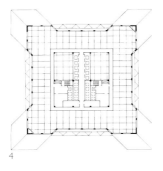

4
5

Lane Crawford Place

■ The shopping complex is built at the prominent junction of Orchard Road's shopping and hotel district in Singapore.

The retail podium block is five stories above and two stories below ground. The second basement floor is linked to the other floors in the junction to complete a pedestrian circuit.

A double-wall system is incorporated into the podium façade to comply with the contradicting design requirements for the podium. Taking into consideration the tropical environment, the stone-clad outer wall has punched openings to provide pedestrians with a shaped walkway. The inner wall, however, has a full-height transparent glass curtain wall that leans over the colonnaded covered walkway to provide the visibility of shopping activities from outside. The unique space created by the double walls is dramatically experienced by both shoppers and pedestrians alike.

The cone-shaped glass atrium is introduced on the corner of the junction to give an identity for the complex. This structure does not only provide an attractive landmark but also serves as an open plaza under its enclosure. The shape of the curtain wall behind the cone is also an inverted cone, and this design feature is reflected in all the other corners. This distinctive shape provides an open plaza under the glazed canopy and works as an inviting entrance for customers.

The high-rise office tower is set toward the rear of the site. It is finished with granite in its lower part to maintain continuity with the podium which is finished with flared granite and polished to give an identity. The upper part is a glass curtain wall expressing a significant degree of contrast with the stone cladding. Due to the local climate, however, it also has a double-glazed system. The outer skin is tinted glass and the inner glass slopes downwards to help reduce the airconditioning load. The top of the tower is finished with aluminum, and to maintain the design integrity of the whole architecture, the cone was designed in a similar manner to the podium corner.

|

Location
Singapore, Republic of Singapore

Completion
1993

Height
985 m

Stories
21 stories, 2 basement levels, and 2 penthouse levels

Area
Site: 7,839 m²; building: 7,839 m²; floor: 58,000 m²

Structure
Reinforced concrete

Architect
Kisho Kurokawa Architect & Associates

Associate architect
Wong & Ouyang (HK) Ltd

Structural engineer
RSP Architects Planners & Engineers

Mechanical engineer
Wong Ouyang & Associates (S) Pte

Client
Wharf Holdings Ltd, Hong Kong

General contractor
Joint venture of Penta Ocean Construction and Low Keng; Huat Construction

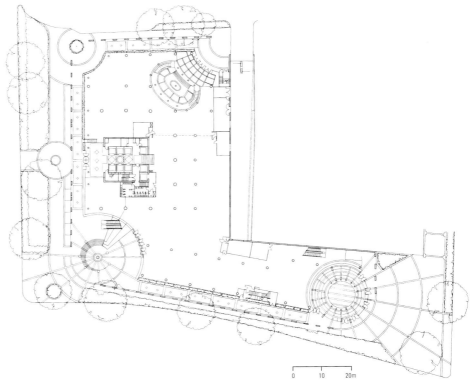

2

3

4

5

1   Overall view to east
2   Walkway between double wall
3   Site plan and ground floor plan
4   Night view
5   Escalator leading to shopping floors
Photography: Shinkenchiku-sha Co., Ltd

0   10   20m

Lee Gardens

■ Anyone who visited the old Lee Gardens Hotel would have been impressed by the spacious and tree-lined urban space created by the building on Hysan Avenue—a rare and much valued outdoor streetscape in the dense urban vicinity of Causeway Bay. The hotel itself, which was patronized by important politicians and Hollywood stars during the two decades of its history, was an important landmark in the area.

In 1992, the Lee family decided to redevelop the hotel and change it into an office building with modern retail and commercial facilities. This created a huge challenge in terms of architectural design: on the one hand, the valued nostalgic quality of the streetscape had to be recreated; and, at the same time, the building, as a landmark of the area, would also need to project the image of a new era.

The configuration of the podium of the new Lee Gardens follows the set-back position of the old hotel along Hysan Avenue, creating a forecourt that serves as both the main entrance hall to the office tower as well as the retail complex. The main entrance hall, which is linked to the office tower lift halls at the third floor by an atrium, was deliberately designed to an average ceiling height of 23 meters, cladded with clear glazing to provide an airy atmosphere and a rich spatial experience for both the interior space as well as the exterior.

A tall wall was designed at the eastern site boundary facing the atrium so as to shield off the undesirable eyesore of illegal structures of the adjacent residential building, and at the same time create an outdoor garden with a water feature that enhances the visual experience as one travels to work daily. On the opposite side of the site a footbridge is provided to connect the shopping arcade with the Caroline Center.

The office tower is strategically located at the eastern part of the site so that a walling effect with buildings at close vicinity can be avoided. The triangular-shaped plan enables two-thirds of the office façade to have a commanding view of Victoria Harbour. Cladded in light silver reflective glass with slender aqueous-color horizontal features, it enhances the feeling of openness and simplicity among other dark green-colored curtain. wall façades of buildings in the vicinity. On the topmost floor is a skygarden that can be used by tenants as a roof garden and at the same time acts as a characteristic feature.

Location
Hong Kong SAR, People's Republic of China

Completion
June 1997

Height
237.38 m with mast; 207.99 m without mast

Stories
51 and 4 basements

Area
Site: 5,591 m²; offices: 66,042 m²; retail: 17,821 m²

Structure
Steel frame: composite structural system of periphery steel frame and central reinforced concrete core wall

Materials
Exterior: silver reflective glazing curtain wall for tower, and granite cladding for podium; interior: granite finish for walls and floors

Use
Commercial

Cost
US$166.7 million

Architect
Dennis Lau & Ng Chun Man Architects & Engineers (HK) Ltd

Structural engineer
Dennis Lau & Ng Chun Man Architects & Engineers (HK) Ltd

Service engineer
Associated Consulting Engineers (E&M Consultants)

Client
Perfect Win Properties Ltd

Main contractor
Aoki Corporation

2

3

4

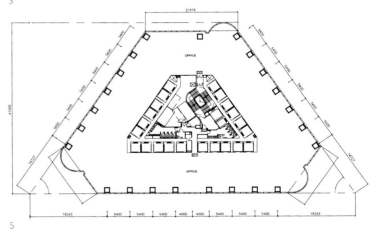

5

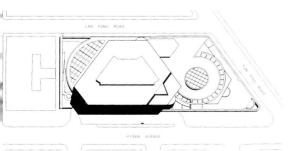

6

1   Lee Gardens and entrance forecourt
2   Atrium with skylight inside shopping arcade
3   Main entrance lobby for office tower
4   Lift hall of office tower at third floor
5   Typical floor plan
6   Site plan
Photography: Frankie Wong & Michael Tse Photography

Lippo Protective Tower

■ The redevelopment of a residential building at 231–235 Gloucester Road in Wanchai into a first-class office tower, added a major new prestigious development to the harborfront. Located at the corner of Canal Road West and Gloucester Road, the development consists of a slender office tower above a carpark podium, with a total gross floor area of 7,640 square meters.

A skylit escalator hall formed adjacent to the tower leads tenants via the Gloucester Road entrance to the spacious main lobby, located on the third floor, from which a fine panoramic sea view can be enjoyed. A water feature, mirrors, and rich stonework create an elegant and spacious entrance experience.

The office tower features an essentially square plan form that has been modified to create popular executive corner offices. A back-service core arrangement optimizes the attractive harbor views. The tower provides 30 office floors, served by three passenger lifts. The floorplan to the upper office floors is marginally reduced in size to create additional column-free corner offices.

The tower is crowned by a stepped, cone-like feature that contains mechanical equipment, and also provides the tower with an appropriate and distinct top, silhouette, and project identity.

The use of silver reflective glass in combination with natural anodized aluminum, held in black aluminum frames, reinforces the sculptural qualities inherent in the design of the tower. The tower is floodlit to celebrate the location and design.

1

Location
Hong Kong SAR, People's Republic of China

Completion
November 1996

Height
155 m

Stories
33

Area
Site: 495 m²; building: 7,650 m²

Structure
Reinforced concrete

Materials
Exterior: aluminum, reflective glass, and granite; interior: aluminum, granite, and French limestone

Use
Commercial

Cost
HK$150 million

Architect
P&T Group

Service engineer (M&E)
Meinhardt (M&E) Ltd

Client
Lippo China Resources Ltd

Contractor
Taisei Corporation

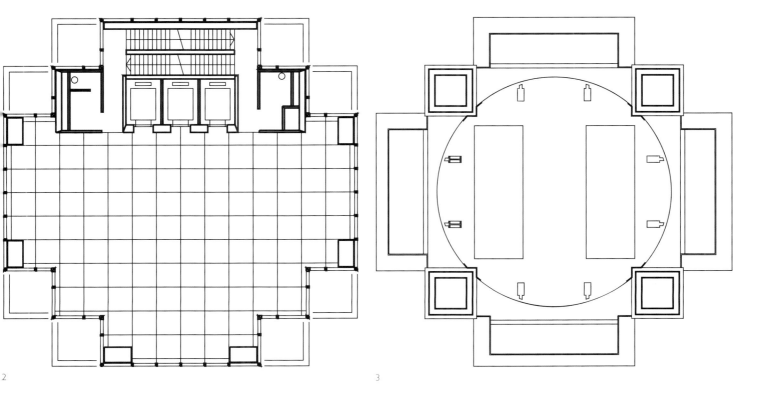

2

3

4

1   View of tower
2   Low zone floor plan
3   Roof plan
4   Spacious main lobby on third floor
Photography: courtesy P&T Group

MBf Tower

■ This tower is a development of the architect's tropical high-rise ideas where the upper parts of the tower have a large two-story high 'skycourt' as the building's key feature that provides better ventilation and deck space ('places-in-the-sky') for plants and terraces.

The lift lobbies are naturally ventilated with bridged walkways leading to the apartment units. Stepped landscaping planter-boxes are located on the main façade of the building.

The site consists of a rectangular-shaped lot along the Julan Sultan Ahmad Shah, Penang. The site is close to Persiaran Gurney and faces the north beach head of Penang. The land is about two miles from the town center and is along the road that links the beach hotels further down in the Tanjung Bungah area to Georgetown.

The structural frame is constructed out of reinforced concrete with slip-form for the service cores and lift shafts. The typical floors are designed column free. The lower block for the apartment is reinforced concrete frame construction with brick infill. The tower columns are located at the periphery of the apartment units and are transferred to the columns at the podium.

1

Location
Penang, Malaysia

Completion
1993

Height
111.1 m

Stories
31

Area
Site: 7,482.39 m²

Structure
Reinforced concrete

Materials
Granite, marble, ceramic tiles, spray tile finishes

Use
Residential

Architect
T.R. Hamzah & Yeang Sdn Bhd

Civil and structural engineer
Reka Perunding LC Sdn Bhd

Client
MBf Holdings Berhad

Contractor
Bina MBf Sdn Bhd

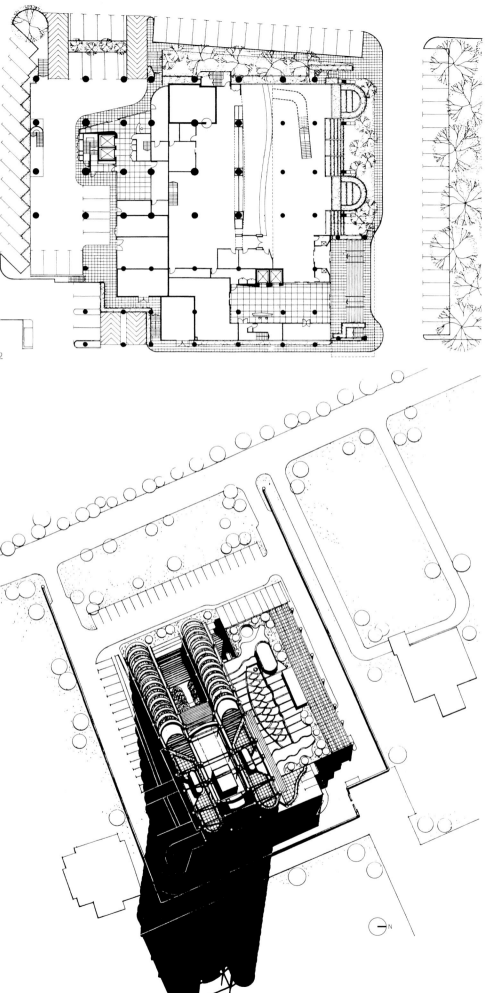

1   Ground floor steel staircase
2   Ground floor plan
3   Site plan
4   East elevation
5   View of passaway of apartment
Photography: courtesy T.R.Hamzah & Yeang Sdn Bhd

Menara 2000

■ The design of this structure was influenced by several requirements of the owner and prospective tenants. Since the building was developed for sale by strata title, there was a need to appeal to the potential purchasers by incorporating the principles of Feng Shui as well as the principles of efficient and cost-effective design. The location of the building relative to the street and to a building across the way was deemed important, in terms of Feng Shui, to its ability to attract tenants. The vertical 'pylon' on the exterior, in addition to serving as a break in the façade through an expression of vertical ribs, is able to collect what is known as 'chi' or a force of energy beneficial to any building. This 'chi' is allowed to enter the building through operable windows within the ribs.

The owners also wanted to reflect on and pay tribute to the Republic of Indonesia, which celebrated its fiftieth anniversary during the year in which the building was being designed and during which construction began. The vertical 'pylon' is thus comprised of five ribs, which allude to the five pillars of pancasila—the foundation of the constitution of Indonesia.

In order to express the core of the building (in structures like this the core is so important to efficient structural design and to the efficient use of the building), the entrance lobby was arranged at street level as a long space parallel to the street, making it three stories in height, and clear glass was used to allow for maximum visibility. The core then becomes evident again at the uppermost levels where it is expressed as the penthouse floors with vertical ribs recalling those of the 'pylon' and contrasting to the horizontal banding of the glass of the tower. The podium contains a mixture of horizontal and vertical expressions, and in an architectural manner alludes to the complicated fabrics of the Indonesian archipelago. The cantilevered entrance canopy with its curving ribs serves as a counterpoint to the extreme verticality of the 'pylon' and as a meeting point of the horizontal and vertical themes.

The tower façade along Jl.Rasuna Said follows the gentle curve of the street, retreating to an orthogonal expression at the other boundaries. Together with setbacks at different floors and at different parts of the building the effect is to create a structure that has a different appearance from every viewing angle.

1

Location
Jakarta, Indonesia

Completion
1997

Height
Building: 149 m; overall: 169 m

Stories
34

Structure
Composite: steel superstructure with reinforced concrete

Use
Offices

Architect
Architects Pacific

Associate architect
PT Arkipuri Mitra

Structural engineer
PT. Perkasa Carista Estetika

MEP engineer
Meinhardt Indonesia

Client/owner
PT. Kalindo Deka Griya

2

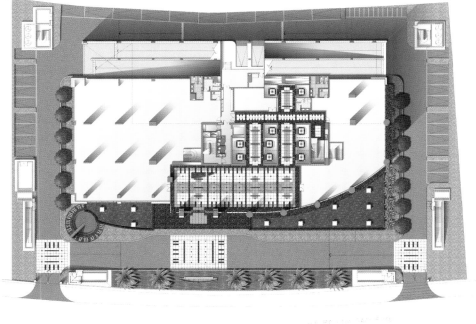

3

1   Building front
2   Entrance lobby
3   Site plan
4   Artist's impression
Photography: courtesy Architects Pacific (2), DR Thomas Prinz (1)

4

Menara Global

■ This building, on a site on Jalan Gatot Subroto along the southern perimeter of the 'Golden Triangle' in south Jakarta, was originally designed as part of a tri-tower development. A twin tower was meant to be constructed opposite the first-phase tower site and a third, larger building was intended for the rear portion of the site, parts of which had not yet been acquired by the developer.

The structure sits on a relatively narrow site with restricted street frontage. Due to the master-planned three-tower arrangement, the entrance to the building is located along its long axis and the core is pushed to the side. A four-story podium of gray granite and reflective glass has been provided so that tenants who require large floorplates, or a mix of retail and food-and-beverage tenants, can be accommodated. The front portion of the tower is curved to visually enlarge the entrance area and to allow the rear tower visibility to Jalan Galot Subroto. The rear of the tower is serrated to allow for more corner offices and to reduce the apparent length of the tower while accentuating the vertical nature of the structure.

As with several other Architecture Pacific buildings, the curtain wall is comprised of vision and spandrel glass with vision glass extending from floor to ceiling. The vision glass has a green hue with silver-tinted spandrel glazing. Maintenance is a central concern of building owners and managers in Jakarta and whenever possible the exterior surfaces have been designed so they can be easily cleaned and, if necessary, replaced.

A large crown of metal ribs has been used at the top of the building to both visually terminate the extruded shape of the main tower and to serve as a shading device for the roof terrace at the penthouse level. The core element extends well beyond the sunscreen/crown and serves as a visual anchor for the tower and as a counterpoint to the horizontality of the crown, alluding to the complexity of the designs and patterns of traditional Javanese batik textiles.

1

2

Location
Jakarta, Indonesia

Completion
1995

Height
Building: 103.60 m; overall: 117.20 m

Stories
22

Structure
Reinforced concrete

Use
Offices

Cost
US$40 million

Architect
Architects Pacific

Associate architect
PT Arkipuri Mitra

Structural engineer
PT. Perkasa Carista Estetika

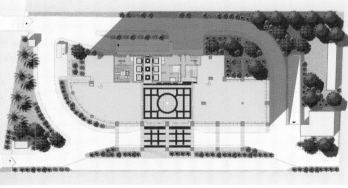

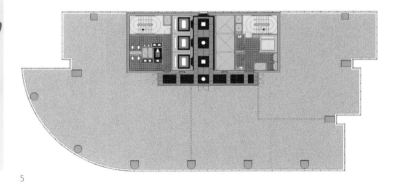

MEP engineer
T. MECO Systech Internusa

Client/Owner
Kanindo/Lippo Group

1 Artist's impression (concept design)
2 View of building
3 Artist's impression of interior (concept design)
4 Site plan
5 Typical floor plan

Photography: courtesy Architects Pacific

Menara Imperium

■ This building was the first major office building in Jakarta to be designed and constructed solely for the strata-title (condominium) market. It was also the first building to be constructed on the site of the Kuningan Persada 'superblock'.

The developer wanted to incorporate a revolving restaurant at the top of the building and this requirement to a large degree determined the shape of the tower. There are only three basement floors, with one devoted almost entirely to retail use, and the balance of the parking is located in the podium five floors above ground. By 'building up' the podium, the first sellable floor is located at level seven, some 25–27 meters above the ground, and hence the views from any sellable floor were a feature of the building. Topping out at over 135 meters in height the building was the tallest strata-title building in Jakarta at the time.

The lobby was designed as a two-story space with a ceiling of translucent plexiglass through which light can pass. Blue and white neon tubes are placed above the ceiling plane allowing the building management to create different moods for different times of the day and year. The floor is polished black granite and the walls are a combination of wavy perforated stainless steel and ribs of plastic with integral backlighting. Through the elevator lobby is a grand stair to the retail spaces on the first basement level.

A health club is located on the sixth floor at the top of the podium, complete with a pool and squash courts. At the top of the building, on the thirty-fifth floor is the revolving restaurant; it offers a panoramic 360 degree view of Jakarta and remains the only one in the city.

The exterior wall is green-blue reflective glass responding to the need for ease of cleaning and a lightweight curtain wall. The glass extends floor to ceiling and with the relatively small floor plate makes for very impressive views from the upper floors.

The structural system is steel using a lightweight system comprised of a concrete shear wall, steel tube columns filled with concrete, and steel plate girders. The total weight of the steel framing is less than 40 kilograms per square meter. The largest perimeter columns are only 750 millimetres in diameter and hence from the inside do not interfere with the views of the tenants while also not taking up very much floor space.

I

Location
Jakarta, Indonesia

Completion
1995

Height
Building: 128.20 m; overall: 134.20 m

Stories
32

Structure
Composite: steel superstructure with reinforced concrete

Use
Offices

Cost
US$40 million

Architect
Architects Pacific

Associate architect
PT Arkipuri Mitra

Structural engineer
Skilling Ward Magnusson Barkshire Inc.

MEP engineer
PT.MECO Systech Internusa

Client/owner
Pacific Metro Realty

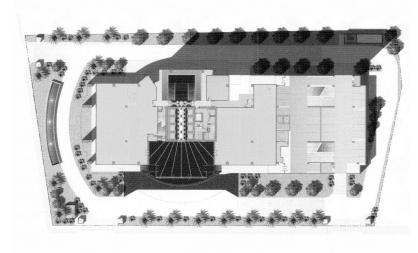

4

1   View of building
2   Entrance lobby
3   South elevation (computer rendering)
4   Site plan
Photography: courtesy Architects Pacific (2), Eric Niemy (1)

Menara Maxis at Kuala Lumpur City Centre

■ Menara Maxis is situated in the northwest corner of the Kuala Lumpur City Centre Development adjacent to the 88-story twin tower office development designed by Cesar Pelli. The front entrance to the site faces the northeast towards the intersection of Jalan Ampang and what will become New City Hall Drive. The back of the site will be the Kuala Lumpur City Centre podium. The building is 51 stories plus three below-grade areas and parking levels.

2

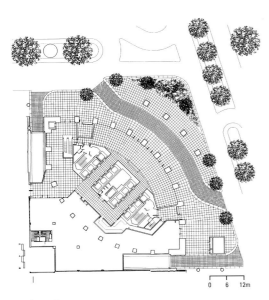

Location
Kuala Lumpur, Malaysia

Completion
1997

Height
204 m

Stories
51 and 3 below-grade

Area
Building: 79,000 m²

Structure
Reinforced concrete frame

Materials
Glass, metal panels, granite

Use
Commercial

Architect
Kevin Roche John Dinkeloo and Associates

Architectural consultant
NRY Architects

Structural engineer
Thorton-Tomasetti Ranh

Mechanical engineer
Jaros, Baum & Bolles, SN

Client
KLCC (Holdings) Sdn Br

Contractor
Cabaran Cota

3

4

1   Ground floor plan
2   Exterior façade
3   Exterior top of building
4   Typical floor plan
Photography: courtesy Kevin Roche John Dinkeloo and Associates

Menara Mesiniaga

■ The building brings together the principles of a bioclimatic approach to the design of tall buildings developed over the previous decade by T.R. Hamzah & Yeang Sdn Bhd.

'Vertical landscaping' is introduced into the building façade and at the 'skycourts'. In this building the planting starts by mounding up from ground level to as far as possible at one side of the building. The planting then spirals upwards across the face of the building with the use of recessed terraces ('skycourts').

A number of passive low-energy features are also incorporated: all the window areas facing the hot sides of the building (east and west) have external louvers as solar-shading to reduce solar heat gain into the internal spaces. Those sides without direct solar isolation (the north and south) have unshielded curtain-walled glazing for good views and to maximize natural lighting.

The lift lobbies on all floors are naturally ventilated and are sun-lit with views to the outside. These lobbies do not require fire-protection pressurization. All stairways and toilet areas are also naturally ventilated and have natural lighting.

The sunroof is the skeletal provision for panel space for the possible future placing of solar-cells to provide a back-up energy source. Building Automation System (BAS) is an active intelligent building feature used in the building for energy saving.

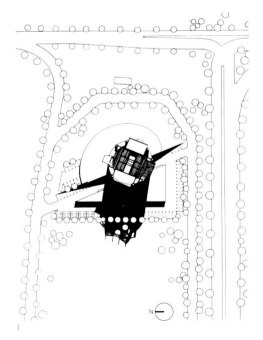

1

2

Location
Selangor, Malaysia

Completion
August 1992

Height
65 m

Stories
14 and 1 basement

Area
6,503 m²

Structure
Reinforced concrete structural frame and brick infill, mild steel truss structure for sunroof, gym roof, and mezzanine deck

Materials
External: laminated float glass, composite aluminum cladding

Use
Offices

Architect
T.R. Hamzah & Yeang Sdn Bhd

Mechanical and electrical engineer
Norman Disney & Young Sdn Bhd

Civil and structural engineer
Reka Perunding Sdn Bhd

Client
Mesiniaga Sdn Bhd

Contractor
Syarikat Siah Brothers Trading (M) Sdn Bhd

3

4

1   Site plan
2   View showing planted ramp
3   Main entrance
4   View of skycourts
5   Second floor plan
Photography: courtesy T.R. Hamzah & Yeang Sdn Bhd

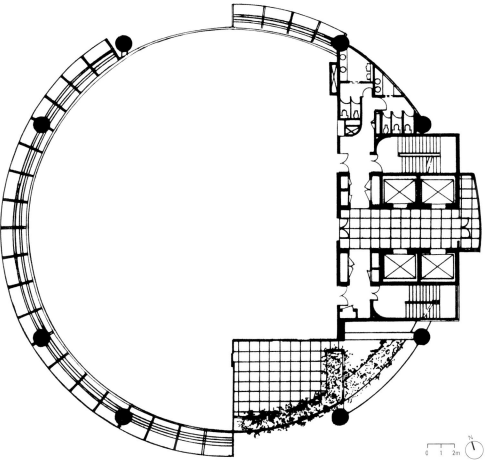

0 1 2m

5

Menara TA1

■ This rectangular site is orientated diagonally north-south, which is not an ideal orientation along latitudes near the equator. The site conditions here are such that the geometry of the site and the geometry of the sun path do not coincide.

The external skin is glazed with a louvered sunshade system on the west but remains unshielded on the north and south corners (since there is minimum solar insulation on these surfaces).

The core, which consists of the lift lobby, toilets, fire stairs, and mechanical and electrical rooms, is located on the east side of the slab, thus keeping the hot sun out of the offices while allowing natural lighting and natural ventilation into the core areas.

The typical internal office floors are column-free and on alternate floors; they open out to a transitional space on the southwest face as an atrium.

Off the atrium are 'steel skycourts' as transitional spaces occur at various alternate levels up the building. A clear maximum span of 18 meters was made possible by the use of prestressed beams.

The communal space at the top of the building is part of the Planning Authority's requirements; it provides space for corporate entertainment. The tensile membrane roof canopy offers protection from the sun and gives the building its landmark status.

The ground entrance lobby is recessed and remains open and naturally ventilated. The tensile membrane entrance canopy provides further protection from sun and rain to the double-volume drop-off point.

Location
Kuala Lumpur, Malaysia

Completion
June 1996

Height
151 m

Stories
37

Area
Site: 4,868.5 m²

Structure
Reinforced concrete structural frame with pre-stressed concrete beams, brick infill

Materials
External: tempered float glass; roof: reinforced concrete on roof terrace, tedlar-coated pvc membrane on painted structure

Use
Offices

Architect
T.R. Hamzah & Yeang Sdn Bhd

Civil and structural engineer
Reka Perunding Sdn Bhd

Mechanical and electrical engineer
Jututera LC Perunding Sdn Bhd

Client
ERF Properties Sdn Bhd

Contractor
Mul-T-plex Engineering (M) Sdn Bhd

2

3

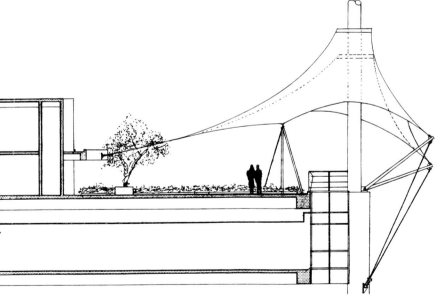

4

1   Façade detail
2   Southeast façade
3   Rooftop canopy
4   Rooftop canopy detail
5   Concept sketches by Paul Matthews
Photography: courtesy T.R. Hamzah & Yeang Sdn Bhd

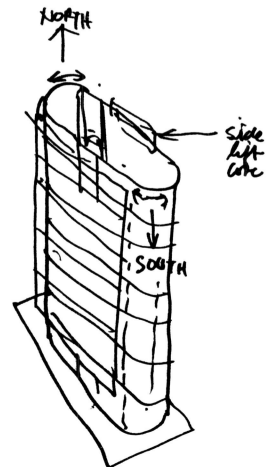

5

Menara Umno

■ The site has an area of about half an acre and is centrally located. The tower is 21 stories and contains spaces for a banking hall at ground level and level one, and an auditorium for meetings and assemblies at level six. The auditorium is also accessible by a separate external staircase. Above this there are 14 floors of office space.

All floors, although designed to be airconditioned, are also naturally ventilated. The building has wind 'wing-walls' to direct wind to special balcony zones that serve as pockets with airlocks (they have adjustable doors and panels to control the percentage of windows that can be opened) for natural ventilation. This building is probably the first high-rise office to use wind as natural ventilation for creating comfort conditions inside a building, as opposed to natural ventilation simply as a source of fresh air supply.

1

2

Location
Penang, Malaysia

Completion
March 1998

Height
93.5 m

Stories
21

Area
1,920 m²

Structure
Reinforced concrete beam and slab construction

Use
Offices

Architect
T.R. Hamzah & Yeang Sdn Bhd

Civil and Structural engineer
Tahir Wong Sdn Bhd

Mechanical and electrical engineer
Ranhill Bersekutu Sdn Bhd

Client/Developer
South East Asia Development Corporation Berhad

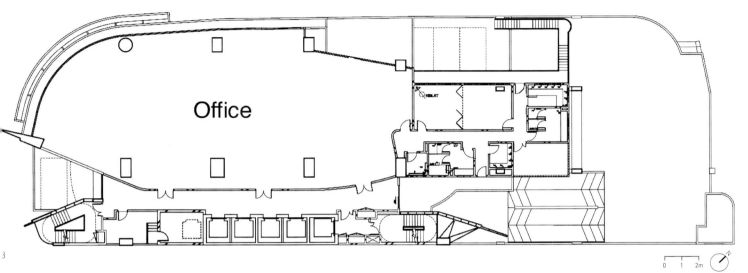

Office

3

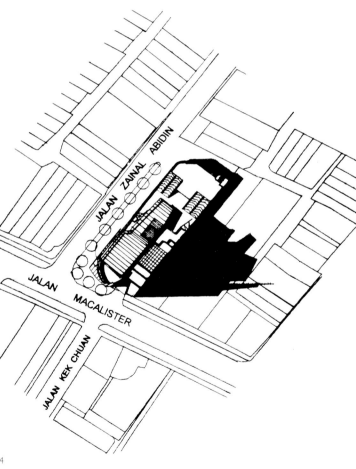

JALAN ZAINAL ABIDIN

JALAN MACALISTER

JALAN KEK CHUAN

4

5

1   Top of wind 'wing-wall'
2   West elevation
3   Typical floor plan
4   Site plan
5   Roof canopy and staircase detail
Photography: courtesy T.R. Hamzah & Yeang Sdn Bhd

The Millenia Singapore Office Buildings and Hotel

■ In the Urban Redevelopment Authority's vision for the city, the Millenia Singapore (includes Millenia Tower, Centennial Tower, and Ritz-Carlton Millenia Singapore) project plays an important and critical role in the development of the city's future master plan. From the central business district, the site is a terminus for an extended axis from the center of the city over Marina Bay, the old historic harbor. The design challenge was to use the site's location effectively to enhance the urban design of the harbor area, yet provide an efficient, economically viable project in a competitive market. The primary elements used to achieve the planning objectives are two office towers and a distinctive hotel.

The hotel, the Ritz-Carlton Singapore, was located to permit sufficient space for a truly magnificent garden entry on the south side and to take advantage of the views of the city. The hotel tower is a single, slender slab, 15 x 106 meters, which stands on the harbor facing the central business district. The guestroom tower floats 15 meters above its base and permits the approaching visitor a glimpse of Marina Bay and the central city, dramatically framed by its supports. The 610 guestrooms of the hotel are enclosed in a granite-clad structure, with large panoramic windows for the guestrooms and octagonal vision windows for the bathrooms, which are placed dramatically on the outside wall.

The tallest element of the composition is a powerfully formed, but simple, office tower capped with a 40 meter, illuminated, pyramid-shaped top. The building, the Millenia Tower, is perched on four 15 meter high illuminated cylinders. It is flanked on two sides by sheets of reflecting water. Sited on axis with the vehicular approach from the airport, it can be seen from a great distance as one approaches the city. The façade is of white granite, perforated with square windows. The top ten stories have, in each corner, projecting octagonal bay windows, which appear to support a truncated, pyramidal top.

A third element in the design is an office building, which relates more particularly to its location on the site. The building, the Centennial Tower, has curved walls roughly facing north and south. The north wall, following the curve of Temasek Avenue leads the eye of the passing motorists to Suntec City and establishes an appropriate urban relationship with that group of buildings.

The two office buildings are located on a large pedestrian plaza bordered on the west by the shopping arcade. In addition the park-like plaza contains sculptures, waterfalls, pools, and trees providing vitality and harmony with the local urban scene.

1

2

Location
Singapore, Republic of Singapore

Completion
1997

Height
Millenia Tower: 176 m; Ritz-Carlton Millenia Singapore: 106 m; Centennial Tower: 136 m

Stories
Millenia Tower: 41; Ritz-Carlton Millenia Singapore: 29; Centennial Tower: 34

Area
Millenia Tower: 83,000 m²; Ritz-Carlton Millenia Singapore: 73,500 m²; Centennial Tower: 50,462 m²

Structure
Concrete

Materials
Granite, glass, and marble

Use
Commercial, hospitality

Architect
Kevin Roche John Dinkeloo and Associates

Associate architect
DP Architects PTE

Structural engineer
Meinhardt (Singapore) Pte Ltd

Service engineer
Meinhardt (Singapore) Pte Ltd

Client
Pontiac Marina Private Limited

Contractor
Dragages et Travaux Publics Architects Pte Ltd

5

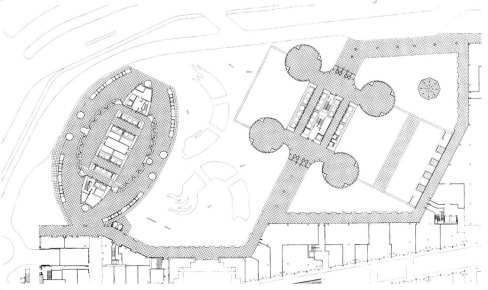

1 Complex exterior Ritz-Carlton front
2 Complex exterior over harbor
3 Plaza fountain at night
4 Plaza fountain and sculpture
5 Entrance canopy at Millenia Tower
6 Site and floor plans of towers

7

8

7   Entrance and lobby of Millenia Tower
8&10   Hotel lobby
9   Entrance to Centennial Tower
11   Aerial Ritz-Carlton pool
12   Ground level Ritz-Carlton pool
Photography: Kevin Roche John Dinkeloo and Associates,
Ritz- Carlton Millenia Singapore (10)

MLC Centre

■ Located in the center of Sydney's business district, the site's 9,130 square meter area resulted from the amalgamation of 23 individual properties. The consolidation took place over a number of years and absorbed a narrow internal street (Rowe Street) in exchange for private land to extend another (Lee's Court). The resulting L-shaped site faces onto the pedestrian area of Martin Place and fronts Castlereagh and King streets.

The major constraint in planning was the existence of the Eastern Suburbs Railway tunnels running diagonally under the site. The tower columns had to be planned to avoid these.

Design studies were directed to enliven the street-level spaces at the base of the inevitably tall office tower, which occupied only 20 percent of the total site. To counter the results of the high development factor, the scheme aims to create open space in the congested center of the city. The resulting privately owned land given over to permanent public use compensates for the intensification of land use.

Because it is located in the retail core of the city, two levels of shopping arcades were required. A podium of plazas was planned on various levels, opening out onto the surrounding streets. Along the boundaries, shops generally face outward, thereby continuing the adjoining existing development, which extends into interior arcades. The central space of the site, however, is open and used for landscaped plazas, outdoor restaurants, and a vertically connecting circular well containing a fountain. There is a cinema, a tavern, various coffee shops, and restaurants, which all open onto some part of the internal pedestrian area of the project.

The tower is square, angled diagonally to avoid the railway tunnels and has blunted corners, resulting in the irregular octagonal plan form.

The tower has a rigid load-bearing core of vertically poured cross-walled concrete. Its exterior is carried by eight heavily loaded massive columns that logically change in plan shape and area from bottom to top, as the loads decrease. For a structure of this height, there is great need for stiffness against lateral wind loads. This is achieved by turning the columns outward at the base and changing their hyperboloid form to become flush with the building façade at the top.

2

Location
Sydney, Australia

Completion
1975

Height
250 m

Stories
67

Area
100,000 m²

Structure
Precast concrete structure

Materials
White quartz exterior

Use
Office building

Architect
Harry Seidler & Associates

Structural engineer
Civil & Civic Pty Ltd and Lehmann & Talty Pty Ltd

Service engineer
Environ Mechanical Services Pty Ltd

Client
Lend Lease Corporation

Contractor
Civil & Civic Pty Ltd

CASTLEREAGH STREET

MARTIN PLACE

0 3 6   N

View of tower from retail center
Glass canopy over tower's entrance escalators
Site plan
Inside Castlereagh and King Street entry
Entry plaza with outdoor restaurants and glass umbrella
View looking up at tower from southeast
Photography: Max Dupain

5

6

National Power Network Control Center

■ The architectural style of this project has taken both traditional architectural culture and the nature of modern architecture into consideration with the use of simple and forthright methods. The design generally obeys the three-section method of classical aesthetics. Using mature modern architectural language, the shape of the building was created by inserting simple volume blocks into one another. The sense of sculpture created by the modeling of the building and the detail treatment of three-story colonnade maintains the solemn character of the building.

Light-colored façade materials were used, and the laminated aluminum panel with a transparent insulation glaze unit and assembled stone panels have created a commercial office building. Metal shades are used on the east- and west-side windows; these not only function as an energy-saving measure by reducing the sunshine, but also serve as an ornament on the façade.

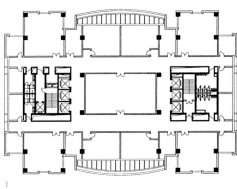

1

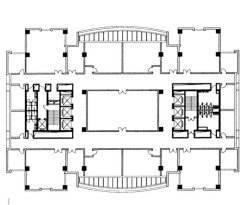

2

Location
Beijing, People's Republic of China

Completion
1999

Height
113.45 m

Stories
28

Area
Building: 50,390 m²; site: 2,850 m²

Structure
Frame shear wall

Materials
Interior: stone, floor tile, paint, timber decoration; exterior: stone, aluminum panel, curtain wall

Use
Office, power network control

Cost
327.15 million RMB

Architect
Architecture Design Institute Ministry of Construction

Client
National Power Network Control Center

Contractor
China Construction 2nd Engineering Bureau

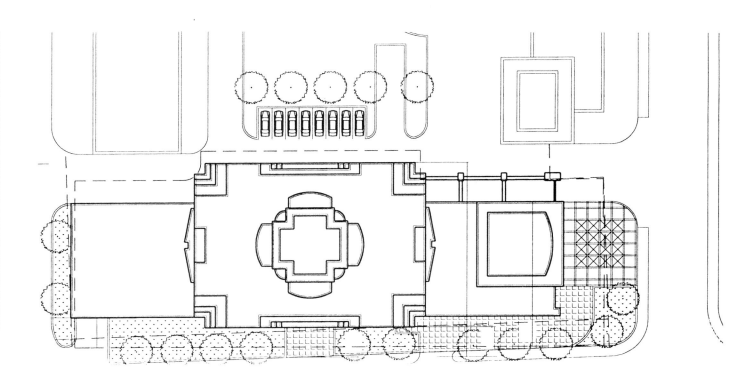

Typical floor plan
East elevation
Site plan
West elevation
Perspective drawing

Photography: courtesy Architecture Design Institute Ministry of Construction

NEC Corporation Headquarters Building

■ Standing 180 meters high, the NEC 'Supertower'—headquarters to the NEC Corporation, one of Japan's leaders in high technology—rises in three distinctive stages above its surroundings in Tokyo's Minato Ward. Emphasis was placed on achieving compatibility with the surroundings, and the low-rise part of the structure was designed to harmonize with the 50 meter skyline formed by the existing buildings. This lower section gives way to a 42 meter wide by 15 meter high opening that serves as a large wind vent by allowing strong, high-level winds deflected down the face of the tower to escape before reaching surrounding buildings or pedestrians on the street.

The mid-level opening also serves as a large window through which daylight enters the atrium and entrance hall located in the low-rise part of the building.

The narrower tower portion, set back from both the lower and mid-levels, houses corporate offices and other facilities.

1

Location
Tokyo, Japan

Completion
January 1990

Height
180 m

Stories
43 and 4 underground

Area
Site: 21,280 m²; building: 6,521 m²; floor: 145,020 m²

Structure
Steel, reinforced concrete

Use
Offices, restaurants, shops, athletic room, multipurpose hall, carpark

Architect
Nikken Sekkei Ltd

Structural engineer
Nikken Sekkei Ltd

Client
NEC Corporation

Contractor
Kajima Corporation, Obayashi Corporation

3

Night view
Evening view
Atrium
Forty-second floor plan
Photography: Hiroshi Shinozawa (2), Satoshi Mishima (1,3, 4)

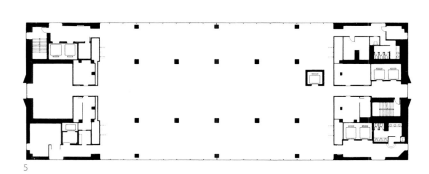

5

Olympia Plaza

■ This commercial development is a 26-story building that occupies an end block. The three abutting streets: King's Road, Power Street, and Electric Street are heavy in both pedestrian and vehicular traffic.

The building design follows a tripartite scheme both in terms of function and appearance. The podium levels consist of shopping arcades; the eight middle levels are restaurant and kitchen areas; and the top 14 floors are office space.

The podium portion consists of two column-free transparent cylindrical forms as display windows. These cylinders are topped with glass blocks to accentuate their importance and to act as beacons at night. The rest of the podium exterior is grids in metal cladding and light box fabric signage.

The restaurant floors are recessed from the site boundary. The Power Street elevation is all clear glazing to allow better views into or from the restaurants. There are also three transparent glass lifts and lift lobbies that look out to the mid-levels of Hong Kong; they are echoed by two triangular forms on the opposite elevation.

The office block takes on an entirely different olive-shaped plan. Each floor is larger than the restaurant floors below and is designed to facilitate large office planning.

Although the tripartite zones all look very distinct, qualities of horizontality, transparency, and being streamline, echo throughout the building to make it a coherent and dynamic form. The design includes horizontality of the podium slabs at the cylinders; recessed grooves in the cladding; trims on the restaurant curtain wall and glass lift enclosure; trims and protruding horizontal bands on the office curtain wall; transparency of the clear glazing; silver-color metal cladding; and the silver reflective curtain wall.

The ground floor of the building is set back to create a wider pavement on Power Street in consideration of the large pedestrian traffic in the area. A canopy has also been provided to shield pedestrians from rain and wind.

1

Location
Hong Kong SAR, People's Republic of China

Completion
September 1999

Height
119 m

Stories
26 and 3 basements (including ground floor and roof)

Area
Building: 26,590 m² (including basement);
site: 1,357 m²

Structure
Reinforced concrete

Materials
Exterior: aluminum cladding; silver reflective insulated glass curtain wall, clear glass wall, glass blocks, fabric signage, aluminum louver

Use
Retail, restaurant, offices, carparking

Cost
HK$425 million

Architect
Wong Tung & Partners Limited

Structural engineer
Joseph Chow & Partners Ltd

Mechanical and electrical engineer
Meinhardt (M&E) Ltd

Developer/Client
Ka Chee Co. Ltd

Main contractor
Gammon Construction Ltd

2

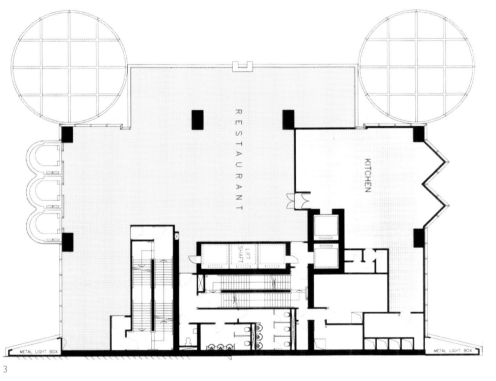

3

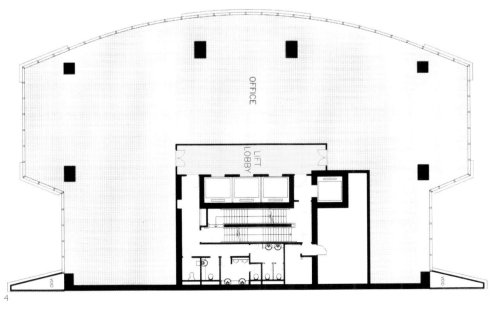

4

5

1 Night view
2 Arcade interior with curvilinear wave ceiling above central
   escalator void
3 Typical restaurant floor plan
4 Typical office floor plan
5 Richly detailed King's Road elevation

Photography: courtesy Wong Tung & Partners Ltd

Osaka Resort City 200

■ Located on the west side of the city center, this multipurpose building complex was developed with the new Land Trust Program of the City of Osaka.

Four blocks of the ORC 200, covering 3 hectares, are placed around a big atrium in the center of the site. Each building is connected with the pedestrian deck at the second-floor level, providing access to the subway station and JR railway station.

One of these twin landmark buildings, soaring 200 meters above street level, is used for the Mitsui Urban Hotel (383 rooms) and offices. The other is for housing (50 stories). A newly developed vibration control device was installed at the top of the hotel and the office tower.

The other two blocks house various facilities for a sports club, a musical hall, a radio station, restaurants, and shops.

1

Location
Osaka, Japan

Completion
March 1993

Height
200 m (without antenna)

Stories
50

Area
Building: 22,687 m²; floor: 252,778 m²; site: 30,123 m²

Structure
Steel frame (hotel and office tower); steel frame and reinforced concrete (residential tower)

Materials
Pre-cast concrete panel with porcelain tile finish and aluminum sash

Use
Public, commercial, hotel, residential, recreational

Cost
¥83,000 million

Architect
Yasui Architects & Engineers Inc.

Associated architect
R.I.A. and Showa Sekkei

Structural engineer
Yasui Architects & Engineers Inc. associated with R.I.A. and Showa Sekkei

Service engineer
Yasui Architects & Engineers Inc. associated with R.I.A. and Showa Sekkei

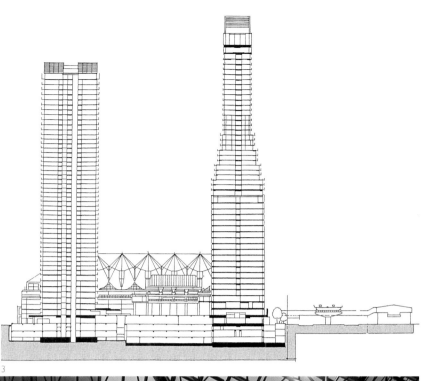

2

3

4

Client
The Daiwa Bank, Ltd; The Sumitomo Trust & Banking
Co., Ltd; The Mitsubishi Trust & Banking Corporation;
The Mitsui Trust & Banking Co., Ltd

Contractor
Simizu Corporation; Haseko Corporation; Konoike
Construction Co.; Takenaka Corporation; Okumura
Corporation

1   Hotel and office tower (south)
2   Night view (north)
3   Section
4   Atrium (pedestrian deck level)
Photography: courtesy Yasui Architects & Engineers Inc.

Osaka World Trade Center Building

(aka Cosmotower)

■ The Osaka World Trade Center Building (WTC) is a key element in the major Technoport Osaka project, promoted by Osaka City. It is part of an extensive new urban center covering 775 hectares, built on three artificial islands in Osaka Bay known as Maishima, Yumeshima, and Sakishima. The WTC is a major landmark in Cosmo Square. The building has a central role in the city's internationalization and as a symbolic landmark in Osaka.

The building height of 252 meters is the tallest in western Japan. It is clad in a reflective glass curtain wall that emphasizes the white structural elements with its mullions, thus accentuating the verticality of the high-rise tower. At the base it widens out in a triangular shape. The low-rise wing, which includes a 69 foot high, all-weather atrium, is known as Fespa. Covering an area of 3,000 square meters, there is ample room for concerts and festivals. Along with the second floor auditorium, the area is part of a lively public space. This second floor auditorium accommodates 380 people and is used for concerts and exhibitions.

The seventh floor houses conference rooms and business support facilities. Floors seven through 44 are office floors equipped with the basic functions for a highly computer-oriented building system. Floor-to-ceiling glazed windows offer panoramic views.

The forty-fifth floor is home of the WTC Museum, featuring photographic exhibitions operated by Japan's International Cooperation Agency. The forty-eighth and forty-ninth floors house the WTC Cosmo Hall, and the Wedding Hall on the forty-ninth floor offers the highest site designed for marriages in Japan. The forty-eighth floor also houses a restaurant, and below, on the forty-sixth and forty-seventh floor, there are seven additional restaurants featuring international cuisine. The fiftieth floor serves as the central facility of the World Trade Center Osaka (WTCO), an international organization offering information to its 400,000 members in major cities around the world.

The top of the building, its fifty-fifth floor, is an observation deck known as the 'Top of the Bay', offering a 360-degree panoramic view. At night the entire building, spilling light from each of its full-height windows on every floor, shines like a 'pillar of light'.

Location
Osaka, Japan

Completion
1995

Height
252 m

Stories
55

Area
Site: 20,000 m²; building: 10,954 m²;
total floor: 149,296 m²

Structure
Steel

Use
Offices

Architect
Nikken Sekkei Ltd and Mancini Duffy Associates

Structural engineer
Nikken Sekkei Ltd and Mancini Duffy Associates

Construction
Obayashi Corp., Kajima Corp., Mitsui Construction Co. Ltd, Kenoike Construction Co. Ltd, Zenitaka Corp., Tokyo Construction Co. Ltd, Okurama Corp., Nishimatsu Construction Co. Ltd, Penta-Ocean Construction Co. Ltd, Nihon Kokudo, Turner JV

Developer
Osaka World Trade Center Building

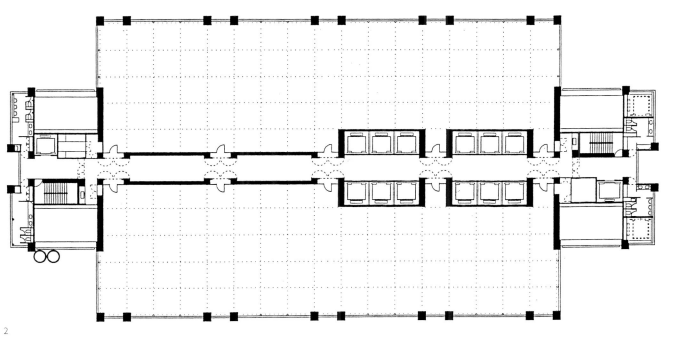

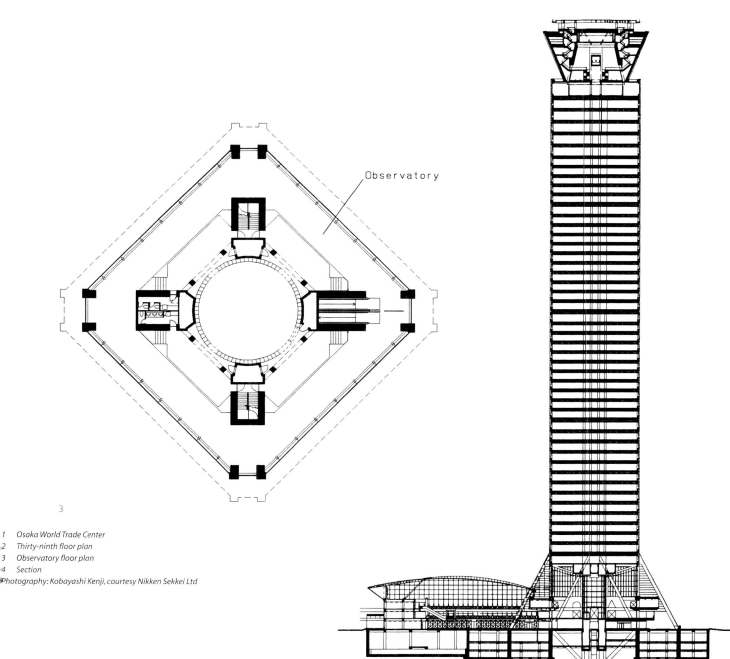

Observatory

1   *Osaka World Trade Center*
2   *Thirty-ninth floor plan*
3   *Observatory floor plan*
4   *Section*
Photography: Kobayashi Kenji, courtesy Nikken Sekkei Ltd

Oterprise Square

(Formerly Titus Square)

■ The site is located at the junction of Nathan Road and Middle Road in Tsimshatsui, a traditionally busy commercial and tourist neighborhood. The site is sandwiched between a number of landmark buildings in the district: the Peninsula Hotel, the Sheraton Hotel, and the Hyatt Regency. It is relatively small in area, only about 1,000 square meters, and what used to be a panoramic view of Victoria Harbour is now largely obstructed by the Sheraton and the newly extended Peninsula Tower.

The redevelopment is envisaged to be a Class-A office building with a retail podium. The challenge to the design was how to fully exploit, under the restrictions of its towering neighbors and its own relatively small area, the potential of the site in this particular 'golden' location.

The strategy in the design of the podium was to introduce a passage cutting diagonally across the site linking Nathan Road and Middle Road. This means that pedestrians are tempted to use this shortcut through the retail areas, and be brought, involuntarily, through the skylit atrium above this passage, into visual contact with the various retail levels and the associated bridgelinks and escalators. As a result, there is an intentional mixing and blurring of the boundary between the private and the public domains, resulting in an architecture that is both fluid and permeable.

In the design of the office tower, a conscious attempt was made to maximize the view of the harbor available at the different levels of the tower. This results in the façade being orientated towards the southwest, from the sixth floor to the thirteenth floor, through the gap between the Sheraton and the Peninsula, and towards the south from the fifteenth floor to twenty-seventh floor, once it is clear of the roof of the Sheraton, to capture the whole panorama of Hong Kong Island.

The form of the building is thus predetermined by the above strategies and represents a distinct example of a 'contextual high-rise' in the dense urban fabric typical of Hong Kong.

1

Location
Hong Kong SAR, People's Republic of China

Completion
1998

Height
108.8 m

Stories
28 and 1 basement

Area
Total floor: 16,463 m²; site: 1,096,906 m²

Structure
Reinforced concrete

Materials
Glass and aluminum

Use
Commercial

Cost
HK$225 million

Architect
Rocco Design Ltd

Structural engineer
Maunsell Consultants Asia Ltd

E/M consultant
Meinhardt (M&E) Ltd

Client
King Tai Development Inc.

Contractor
Penta Ocean Construction Ltd

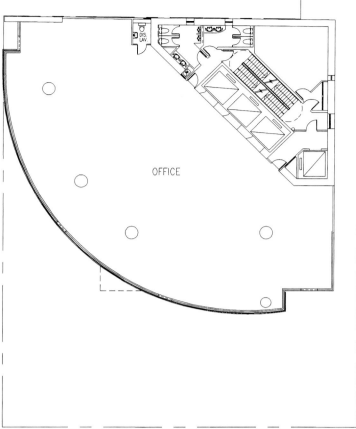

2

3

4

1   Exterior view
2   View of building in context
3   Floor plan (levels 8–13)
4   View looking up at atrium passage
5   View looking out from atrium passage
Photography: courtesy Rocco Design Ltd and ART Commercial
Workshop

5

Oversea-Chinese Banking Corporation Centre (OCBC)

■ This 52-story building occupies a focal position in the emergence of modern Singapore, where it was undertaken in partial realization of a master plan for the redevelopment of Raffles Place as a crossroads of international commerce. Located on the edge of the Singapore river at the hub of the 'Golden Shoe' (the traditional center of Chinese commerce), OCBC has served as a vertical anchor for the developing cityscape.

The client requested a new headquarters building on the site of its former main offices that would establish a unique identity on both the skyline and at street level. The new facility was to house an imposing ground floor banking hall, and provide some half a million square feet of office space, largely for the bank but also for tenant leasing. The solution involves a 194 meter high tower (the tallest building in Southeast Asia upon completion in 1976) designed with an innovative structural system to create a bold, yet serene image.

Unlike other towers with a single, centrally located service core, OCBC has twin concrete cores at either end of the building. The system depends on a structural concept similar to a ladder in which steel trusses and prestressed concrete girders span between the cores, acting as rungs, to transfer gravity loads through the cores to the foundations. The most important rungs, or primary transfer trusses, occur at the forth, twentieth and thirty-fifth floors where three tiers of column-free office floors are 'floated' between the cores. Each tier is articulated by a cast-in-place concrete sunscreen which, cantilevered 5.5 meters out from the building, is faced in glass mosaic tile to match the off-white granite that clads the semi-circular cores. Aside from their role in supporting the office floors, the two cores enclose all of the building's 29 elevators, its HVAC systems, and the radial elevator lobbies that service each floor.

The bi-core structural system allows the building base to be opened up as a vast banking hall, 53 meter long by 36.5 meters wide, unobstructed by interior supports. A 12 meter high glazed enclosure defines this 1,300 square meter room and transforms its apparent mass into volume. Boundaries between interior and exterior are thus intentionally blurred as the presence of the bank extends out to the street through the transparent façades. To the east, a garden plaza further mitigates architectural mass as a 12 meter long bronze—the largest walk-through structure ever created by Henry Moore—contrasts playfully with the strong tower form and animates public space.

1

Location
Singapore, Republic of Singapore

Completion date
1976

Height
194.46 m

Stories
52

Area
Building: 86,300 m²

Structure
Office: steel trusses between slip-formed reinforced concrete end cores with concrete slabs and beams construction

Materials
Exterior: granite

Use
Bank Headquarters and Investment Office Building with carpark

Cost
US$36 million

Architect
I.M. Pei & Partners

Structural engineer
Ove Arup & Partners, Mueser, Rutledge, Wentworth & Johnson

Mechanical/Electrical engineer
Preece, Cardew & Rider, Cosentini Associates

Client
OCBC Centre

General contractor
Morrison-Knudsen International Co. Inc. and Low Keng Huat Construction Co. (S) Pte Ltd

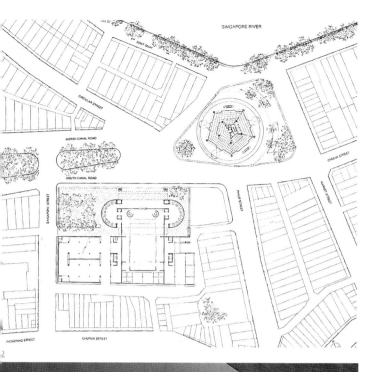

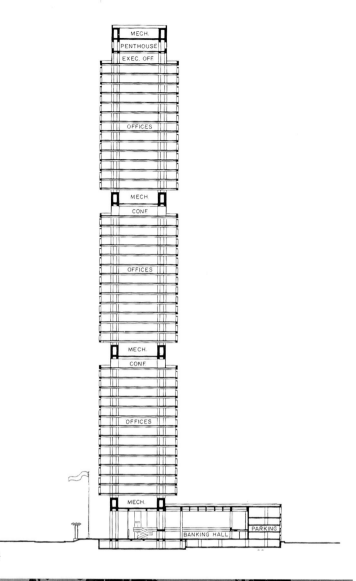

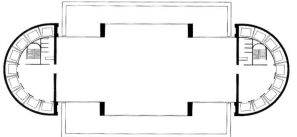

View between Fuller building and bridge
Site plan
Façade detail: three packages and service core, skyward view
Section
Northeast elevation of Singapore Harbor, 1976
Typical floor plan
Photography: courtesy Pei Cobb Freed & Partners; Shang Wei Kouo
(1, 3), Wayne Thom (5)

Pacific Place

■ Pacific Place, one of the largest comprehensive developments in Hong Kong, includes a major shopping centre, three hotels, apartments, and office blocks, with a total gross floor area of over 490,000 square meters.

Pacific Place was developed in two phases because the site was acquired at two separate land auctions. The JW Marriott Hotel, the Atrium Apartments, One Pacific Place, and The Mall Phase I comprise the first phase of the development. The second phase includes the Island Shangri-La Hotel, the Hotel Conrad Hong Kong, the Parkside Apartments, Two Pacific Place, and The Mall Phase II. Planning for the first phase was already well advanced when it became necessary to incorporate the second and larger acquisition.

Restraint was exercised in the choice of cladding and glazing materials in order to achieve visual harmony between the four towers.

1

2

Location
Hong Kong SAR, People's Republic of China

Completion
1988/1991

Height
164 m to 237 m (including basement)

Stories
One Pacific Place: 36; Two Pacific Place/Island Shangri-La: 56; JW Marriott Hotel: 46; Conrad Hong Kong: 53

Area
Building: 490,000 m²; site: 6.5 ha

Structure
Reinforced concrete and structural steel columns

Materials
Interior: granite

Use
Commercial, retail, hotel, apartments

Cost
Phase I: HK$800 million; Phase II: HK$2,200 million

Architect
Wong & Ouyang (HK) Ltd

Civil and structural engineer
Wong & Ouyang (Civil-Structural Engineering) Ltd

Electrical and mechanical engineer
Wong & Ouyang (Building Services) Ltd

Lighting
Corbett Design Associates Ltd; Wheel Gersztoff Friedman

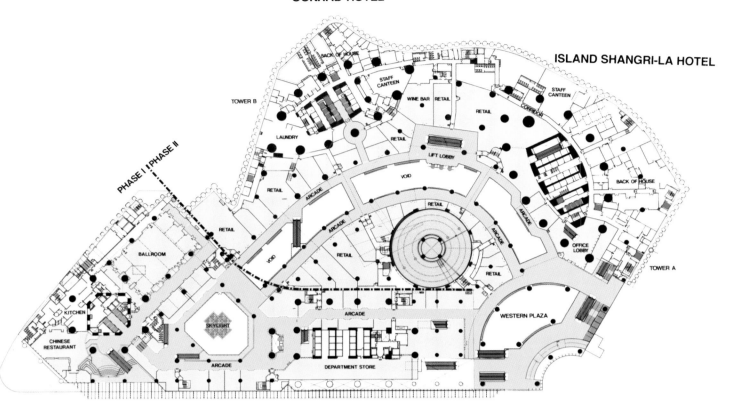

CONRAD HOTEL

ISLAND SHANGRI-LA HOTEL

TOWER B

PHASE I | PHASE II

BACK OF HOUSE

STAFF CANTEEN

WINE BAR RETAIL

STAFF CANTEEN

LAUNDRY

RETAIL

RETAIL

CORRIDOR

LIFT LOBBY

RETAIL

BACK OF HOUSE

VOID

RETAIL

ARCADE

ARCADE

RETAIL

ARCADE

VOID

ARCADE

RETAIL

RETAIL

ARCADE

RETAIL

OFFICE LOBBY

BALLROOM

RETAIL

VOID

TOWER A

KITCHEN

SKYLIGHT

RETAIL

WESTERN PLAZA

CHINESE RESTAURANT

ARCADE

ARCADE

DEPARTMENT STORE

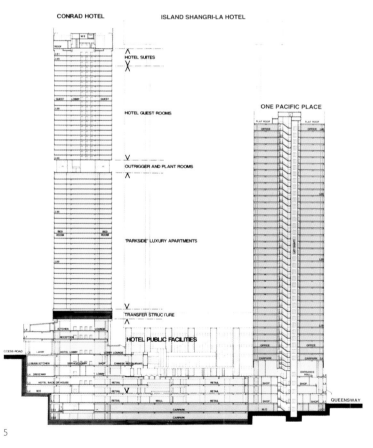

CONRAD HOTEL

ISLAND SHANGRI-LA HOTEL

HOTEL SUITES

HOTEL GUEST ROOMS

ONE PACIFIC PLACE

FLAT ROOF OFFICE

FLAT ROOF OFFICE

OUTRIGGER AND PLANT ROOMS

'PARKSIDE' LUXURY APARTMENTS

OFFICE

OFFICE

TRANSFER STRUCTURE

HOTEL PUBLIC FACILITIES

OFFICE

OFFICE

CARPARK

CARPARK

ENTRANCE HALL

QUEENSWAY

MALL

CARPARK

CARPARK

5

Landscape
...elt Collins & Associates

...lient
...wire Properties Ltd

...ontractor
...hase I: Shui On Construction Ltd.; Phase II: Dragages
...: Travaux Publics (HK) Ltd

1   Level 4 Landscape Plaza
2   Aerial view
3   Plan at level 3
4   Two Pacific Place
5   Diagrammatic section

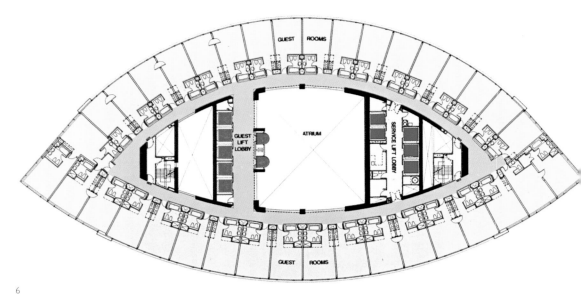

6

7

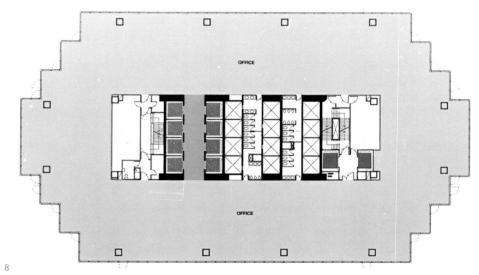

8

9

6   Island Shangri-La Hotel typical floor plan
7   Hotel lobby
8   Pacific Place typical floor plan
9&10   The mall
11   Hotel Conrad typical floor plan
12   JW Marriott Hotel typical floor plan
13   Hotel lobby
14   JW Marriott Hotel
Photography: courtesy Wong & Ouyang (HK) Ltd

10

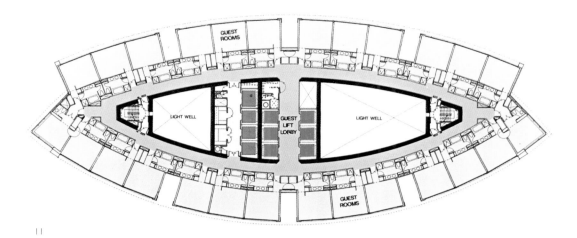

11

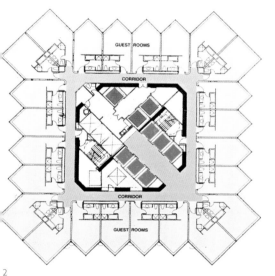

12

3

14

Pengnian Plaza

■ Pengnian Plaza, in the center of Shenzhen, is in an advantageous geographical position that makes it possible to share prominence in the city together with the World Trade Center, the Development Center, and the Sunlight Hotel. The project comprises four high-rise buildings, including the 48-story Yu's Hotel with a three-story podium, the 30-story Xiangshi building, and Xingmao building with two three-story podiums. The whole building group, while being connected together by podiums above the ground, has four levels of basement under the ground. It provides a total floor area of 180,000 square meters.

The first thing was to integrate the building group into the urban environment. Therefore, the main high-rise building, chosen as the focus for landscape creation, was placed in the prominent position of a street intersection, 45 degrees facing the crossing point of two main thoroughfares. This design, while adding a new landmark to the city, helps boost the name of the property owner. Also, as the existing building on the south side of the street has a recessed small plaza facing the intersection, Yu's Hotel has its podium projected forward to borrow the space and create another small plaza. The plazas, in fact, offer a spatial transition from the urban surroundings to the buildings, expanding the usable area around them and making the space less crowded.

Because the four high-rise buildings under the project belong to four different owners, it is important to set the properties apart for easy management, but not to compromise on their functions and an overall architectural conformity. To achieve this, the upper parts of the buildings are separated from each other entirely, while their podiums are connected together on the exterior. Their underground parking lots are centralized, while their utility rooms are isolated. In appearance, the podiums are the bond that holds the buildings as a group, the focus is Yu's Hotel, and the sophisticated complex is arranged in a simple way to form a clear-cut, tall, and straight skyline. In addition, a group of subtle arc lines curving in different directions decorate the buildings, creating a Baroque flavor in the architectural expression.

1

Location
Shenzhen, People's Republic of China

Completion
1999

Height
222 m

Stories
56 and 4 underground

Area
Building: 135,300 m²; site: 13,900 m²

Structure
Frame-tube; shear wall

Materials
Interior: stone, floor tile, paint; exterior: stone; curtain wall: tile

Use
Hotel, offices, commercial

Cost
161.87 million RMB

Architect
Architecture Design Institute Ministry of Construction

Client
Fok Wah (Shengzhen) Real Estate Development Co. Ltd

Contractor
5th Division of 1st Jiangsu Provincial Construction Company

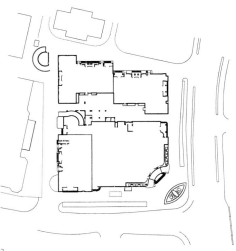

3

4

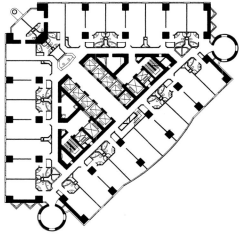

5

1   Side view
2   Whole view
3   Site plan
4   Ground floor plan
5   Hotel typical floor plan

Photography: courtesy Architecture Design Institute Ministry of Construction

Peninsula Bangkok

■ Brennan Beer Gorman / Architects was selected in an international competition to design the 40-story Peninsula Hotel Bangkok. The five-star hotel was designed to create an exciting addition to the city's skyline. Like New York, London, and Paris, Bangkok's identity is tied to its river, and the client's brief required that all guestrooms be no less than 6 meters wide and offer a view of the Chaophraya River.

The dominant feature of the project is the hotel tower's unique symmetrical double 'V' design. The single-loaded corridor design provides each of the 400 guestrooms and suites the requisite river views while increasing the flood of natural light into the corridors. The design also maximizes the amount of linear square footage, resulting in a more compact and efficient building.

The entrance drive rises gently from the natural grade of the landscaped site, terminating in a paved courtyard with central canopy. The ballroom, meeting, and prefunction rooms are situated to the west of the courtyard and are linked to the hotel's main lobby from a two-story shopping arcade.

A grand two-story lobby includes the front desk registration, lobby lounge, and Thai restaurant, all with commanding views of the river. A separate lobby bar is located adjacent to the main entry. Additional food and beverage facilities are on the ground level, linked visually and physically to the lobby by a grand open stair. At the center is a Chinese restaurant overlooking the spacious, landscaped grounds and river. An all-day restaurant is located on the southern side of the grounds, with wonderful river and garden views.

Outdoor recreation facilities include a pool, pool terrace, snack bar, tennis courts, and an indoor squash court.

The remainder of the ground floor contains the hotel's back-of-the-house facilities. The first floor has been developed as a mezzanine overlooking the lobby and includes the administration, business center, and River View meeting room and boardroom.

There are 33 typical guestroom floors with 12 keys per floor, including two 84 square meter (898 square foot) suites located at the point of the 'V'. Typical guestrooms measure 54 square meters (577 square feet). The thirty-fifth floor contains a dramatically scaled presidential suite. Five high-speed passenger elevators and four service elevators service guest floors.

Location
Bangkok, Thailand

Completion
November 1998

Height
125 m

Stories
40

Materials
Steel reinforced concrete, granite at podium

Use
Hotel

Design architect
Brennan Beer Gorman / Architects

Executive/associated architect
RMJM

Client
Siam Chaophraya Holdings Company (a joint venture between the Phatara-Euromill Group of Thailand and Shanghai Hotels Ltd)

Contractor
E.C. Harris (construction manager)

2

3

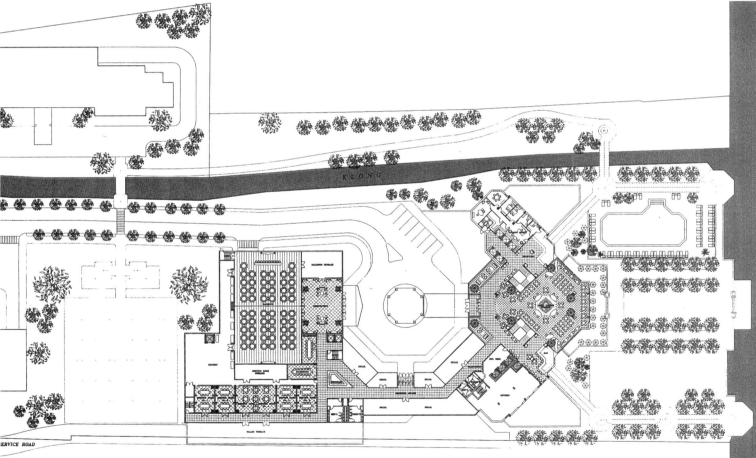

4

1   Peninsula Bangkok
2   Eastern façade viewed from across Chaophraya River
3   Main entrance
4   Schematic site plan
Photography: courtesy Peninsula Bangkok

Petronas Towers at Kuala Lumpur City Centre

■ Malaysia is among the fastest emerging industrialized countries in the Pacific Basin. To meet the demand of urban growth for Kuala Lumpur, its federal capital, the Malaysian Government decided to allow the Selangor Turf Club and its surrounding land, strategically located in the heart of the commercial district the Golden Triangle, to be developed into a new 'city-within-a-city'.

Approximately half of the site is devoted to public areas of park and garden surrounded by 18 million square feet of commercial, retail, hotel, recreational, and residential development.

Phase I of the Kuala Lumpur City Centre development includes the twin 88-story Petronas Towers; two other office towers of retail/entertainment facilities; and below-grade parking and service facilities for 5,000 cars. Public functions within the complex include a Petroleum Discovery Centre, an art gallery, the 850-seat Dewan Petronas Filharmonik concert hall, and a state-of-the-art multimedia conference center. A multi-story shopping and entertainment galleria connects the office towers at the base, integrating the entire complex.

The two Petronas Towers are connected by a skybridge at the sky lobby levels (forty-first and forty-second floors) to facilitate inter-tower communication and traffic. Organized around this interchange of the circulation system are shared Petronas facilities such as the conference centre, the upper surau (prayer room), and the executive dining room.

The lobby core wall finish is light-colored Malaysian woods within a stainless steel grid. The lobby marble floor pattern is derived from one of the most popular Malaysian Pandan weaving and bertam palm wall matting patterns. The wall and floor marble colors are different for the two lobby levels to reinforce the sense of orientation required by the double-deck elevator system. To minimize the contrast of brightness between the exterior and interior, a continuous wooden screen wall shields the perimeter of the lobby wall, reinforcing the sense of the tropical locale and optimizing the use of Malaysian crafts.

The crescent-shaped mall of the retail/entertainment complex has a total of 1.5 million square feet of retail, food, and entertainment facilities located on six levels (concourse through to level five). The design of the exterior, using color ceramic tiles, reflects the richness and multiplicity of the Malaysian culture. Arcades and canopies at street level enhance pedestrian comfort, evoking the 'five-foot way' commonly found in traditional shop houses.

1

Location
Kuala Lumpur, Malaysia

Completion
1998

Height
Towers: 451.9 m above street level;
pinnacle: 73.575 m

Stories
88

Area
218,000 m² each tower

Structure
A core and cylindrical tube frame system constructed entirely of cast-in-place high-strength concrete (up to grade 80); floor framing at tower levels is concrete fill of conventional strength on composite steel floor deck and composite rolled steel framing

Cladding
Horizontal ribbons of vision glass and stainless steel spandrel panels. 85,000 m² of cladding area above level six

Use
Offices, retail/entertainment

Architect
Cesar Pelli & Associates Inc.

Design principal
Cesar Pelli FAIA

Associate architect
Adamson Associates

Architect-of-record
KLCC Berhad Architectural Division

Structural engineers
Thornton-Tomasetti Engineers and Ranhill Bersekutu Sdn Bhd

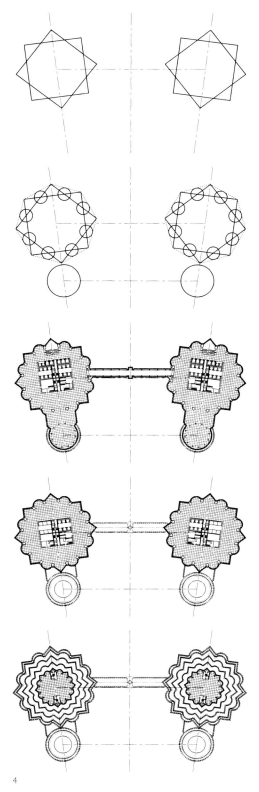

MEP engineers
Flack + Kurtz and KTA Tenaga Sdn. Bhd

Landscape design
Balmori Associates, NR Associates and Selangor

Client
Kuala Lumpur City Centre (Holdings) Sdn Bhd

1   General view seen from public park
2   Site plan
3   View up from entrance
4   Generating geometry of tower floorplate
5   View of towers on skyline at sunset

Photography: courtesy Cesar Pelli & Associates Inc. (3), Jeff
Goldberg/Esto (5); L. Ng/CP&A (2); G. Binder/courtesy Buildings
& Data s.a. (1)

Post and Telecommunications Tower

■ Based upon the geometry of a rotating square, this 26-story, 180 meter high tower in the Chinese city of Tenjing combines the functions of telecommunications repeater, telecommunications staff training center, and office building.

Clad in glass curtain walling with aluminum spandrel panels, the structural frame is a combination of steel and reinforced concrete. The total floor area of the building is 45,000 square meters. The lower podium stories are differentiated from the tower by being finished in clay tiles. The podium roof also serves as a garden.

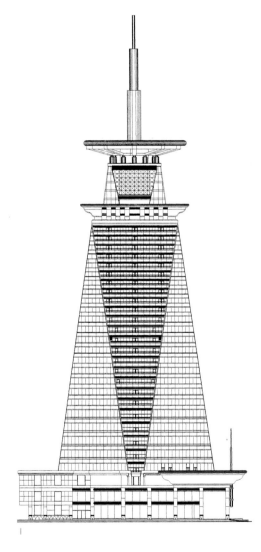

1

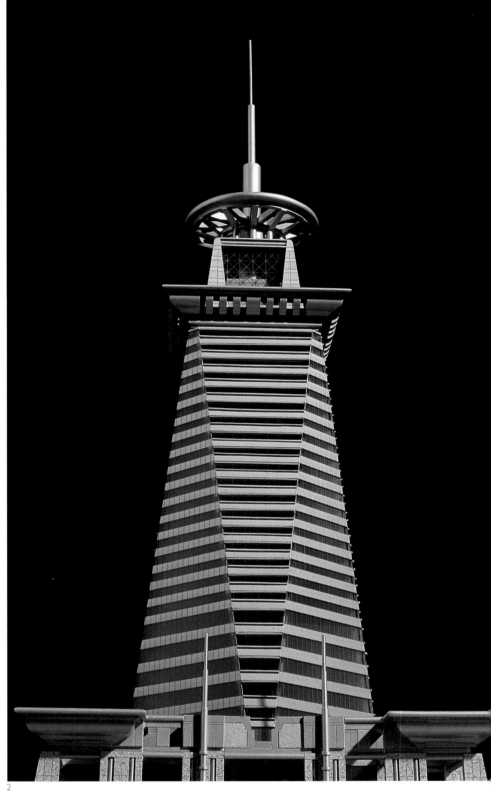

2

Location
Tenjing, People's Republic of China

Completion
1997

Height
180 m

Stories
26 and 2 basements

Area
Site: 1,800 m²; floor: 45,000 m²

Structure
Reinforced concrete

Materials
Granite

Use
Offices

Cost
US$36 million

Architect
C.Y. Lee & Partners, Architects & Planners

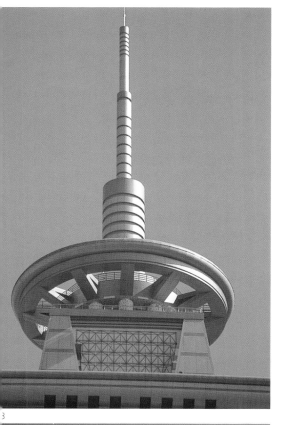

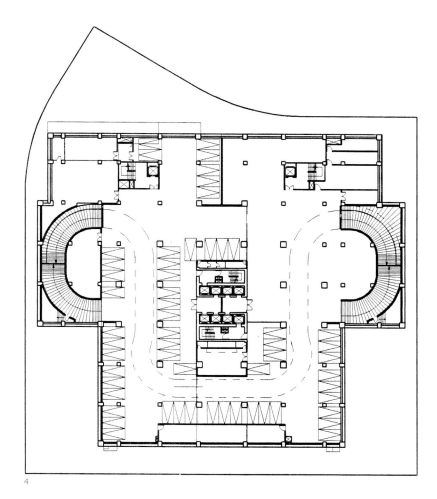

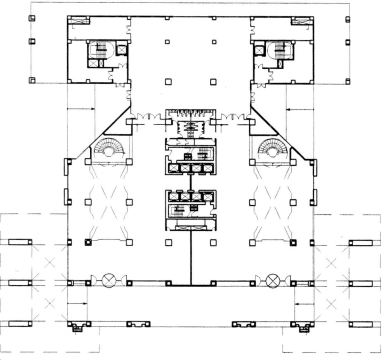

1   Side elevation
2   Model
3   Spiral
4   Basement floor plan
5   Front elelvation
6   First floor plan
7   Rooftop
Photography: courtesy C.Y. Lee & Partners, Architects & Planners

Republic Plaza

■ This high-rise building is located at Raffles Place in the central business district of Singapore. The most important architectural feature of this building is its octagonal sections created by cutting off corners from squares of the high-rise tower. The designer of the building wanted to create an effect like that of the facets of a high-quality diamond.

The size and shape of the site also had a significant impact on the eventual design. To emphasize the unique character of the site and to contribute as much to the urban development of the area as possible, most of the surrounding site space was allocated as walkways.

The entrance hall to the multi-story section is a four-story open atrium in appropriate scale to the Raffles Place Park and the urban scale of the surrounding streets.

The cut-off corners of the high-rise floors are designed to create a gentle impression and to produce an auspicious shape according to Chinese Feng Shui or geomancy.

On the lower portions of the tower, the long sides of the octagon are aligned with the streets whereas in the upper portions, the sides are rotated through 45 degrees to improve the view of the harbor and the sea for the tenants.

The highest point of the 66-floor building is 280 meters, making it one of Singapore's highest skyscrapers. The tower is made up of three portions, each narrower than the last, creating a perspective that emphasizes the building's height. The idea of a central core plan was adopted for Republic Plaza to enhance the view from the office floors and maximize the versatility of the space for rent.

The exterior walls are a combination of polished granite, blue-tinted reflective glass, and black-colored mullions. According to the designer, the polished granite is intended to express stability and eternity while the glass expresses a contemporary mood.

The curtain wall surrounding the four sides is gradually inclined to accommodate changes in the floor area.

Location
Singapore, Republic of Singapore

Completion
January 1996

Height
280 m

Stories
66 and 1 basement

Area
Site: 6,765 m²; building: 4,887 m²; floor: 122,781 m²

Structure
Steel frame, reinforced concrete

Use
Office and commercial (retail shops and restaurant)

Cost
S$251.4 million

Architect
RSP Architects Planners & Engineers (Pte) Ltd

Design architect
Kisho Kurokawa Architect & Associates

Structural engineer
RSP Architects Planners & Engineers (Pte) Ltd

Mechanical engineer
Squire Mech Pte Ltd

Quantity surveyor
Rider Hunt Levett & Bailey

Supervisors
RSP Architects Planners & Engineers (Pte) Ltd

Client
CDL Properties Pte Ltd

General contractor
Shimizu Corporation

2

3

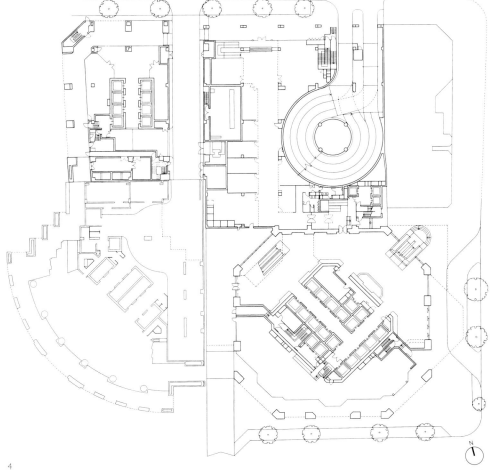

1   External façade
2&3   Main lobby
4   First floor plan
Photography: Shinkenchiku-sha Co., Ltd

4

Rinku Gate Tower

■ The Rinku Gate Tower North Building, or the Airport Gate Tower North Building, was planned as the core structure of a new 'airport town' (the Kansai International Airport); it is situated to face two separate sites, with the railway and the road to the airport in between. This building was constructed as the phase one work of the twin high-rise building construction project.

The building has 56 stories above ground and rises 256 meters. Its facilites include a conference hall and rooms, hotel, clinic, fitness club, offices, information center, and restaurants. Of all these facilities, the hotel and conference hall are especially important as they are designed to support international business occasions.

The hotel, which has an entrance lobby (first floor through to the fourth floor), banquet rooms, 361 guestrooms (twenty-ninth through to the fiftieth floor), and sky restaurant (fifty-second to fifty-fourth floor), has an air of grace, sophistication, splendor, and comfort, which is a result of the design concept incorporating Japanese modernity with Western colors. This concept aims at creating a high-quality space where what is purely Japanese is felt casually while the universality of an international hotel is maintained.

The large conference hall on the sixth floor is able to accommodate 650 people, and is equipped with a four-language simultaneous interpretation facility, a large size video projector, and so on, making it capable of accommodating regular international conferences. In addition, there are 10 small and large conference rooms. The hall and rooms are mostly finished in wood, cloth, and carpet to create spaces with a natural and restful atmosphere.

1

Location
Osaka, Japan

Completion
August 1996

Height
256 m

Stories
56 and 2 underground

Area
Site: 16,870 m²; building: 14,100 m²; floor: 118,047 m²

Structure
Steel, reinforced concrete

Use
Conferences, hotel, offices

Architect
Nikken Sekkei Ltd

Structural engineer
Nikken Sekkei Ltd

Service engineer
Yasui Architects & Engineers, Inc.

Client
Rinku Gate Tower Building Co. Ltd

Contractor
Obayashi Corporation, Takenaka Corporation, Kajima Corporation, Schal Bovis, Inc., Okumura Corporation, Konoike Construction Co. Ltd, Toda Corporation, Haseko Corporation, Asanuma Corporation, Muramoto Corporation, Daisue Corporation, Morimoto Corporation, Nankai Tatsumura Construction Co. Ltd

2

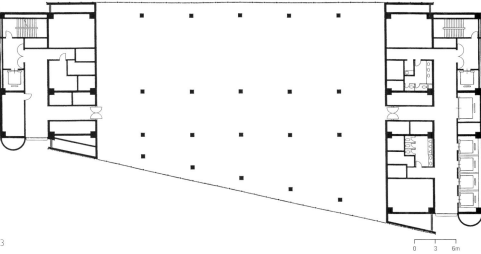

3

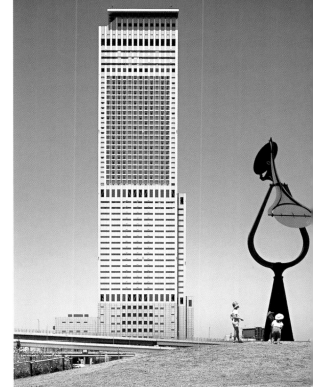

0 3 6m

1   Exterior view
2   Conference hall
3   Typical floor plan (upper level)
4   Elevation
Photography: courtesy Nikken Sekkei Ltd, Kiyohiko Higashide (1, 2)

4

Riverside Development (Stage 1)

■ The first stage of this two-stage project is complete. It is built on a 2 hectare site fronting Brisbane's riverfront at one end of the city's business center.

Previously blocked off by a continuous wall of low buildings and wooden wharves, the location offered the opportunity for the development to open up the river's edge and make it accessible to the city. Construction was permitted to extend into the water, but covered space had to be provided for a future water-edge expressway below. Ferry wharves and a marina for private yachts was also planned.

The Brisbane Stock Exchange is housed in the base of the tower and provision was made for restaurants, banks, shops, and an underground carpark for 500 cars. Planning allowed for a second stage, originally for a hotel but later changed to offices.

Plan forms for both stages were evolved to take the greatest advantage of direct water views. Most square, round or rectangular central core plans (usually the most efficient for high-rise office towers) were discarded as offering limited water views in favor of a triangular plan, which not only faced more than two-thirds of offices to the water but did so up and down the river's length. Water outlook was effective even from top floors, which would otherwise look straight across the river. The shape also preserved and respected the views from a second stage without impairing privacy between the buildings.

On the waterfront a large public space is defined by lower buildings that surround the tower. A wide opening towards the riverfront is left framed by a huge curved connecting bream defining the open plaza. Steps lead down to the water under this opening, traversed by a series of ramps ('stramps'), which provide the required disabled access to the public ferry wharves. This public access to the water will be extended in the future on both sides beyond the site to form a continuous waterfront promenade.

Location Brisbane, Australia	**Structure** Concrete structure, granite facing	**Structural engineer** Rankine & Hill
Completion 1986	**Materials** Polished granite, tinted glass, aluminum sunblades	**Service engineer** Environ Mechanical Services Pty Ltd
Height 120 m	**Use** Offices	**Client** Civil & Civic Pty Ltd
Stories 40	**Cost** AUD$120 million	**Contractor** Civil & Civic Pty Ltd
Area Net office space: 50,000 m²; floor: 1,500 m²	**Architect** Harry Seidler & Associates	

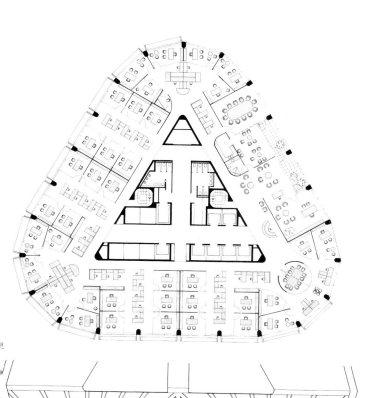

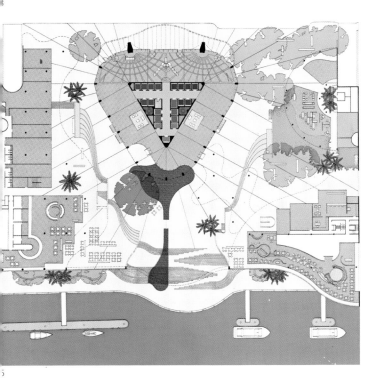

5

6

1 View across the harbor
2 Typical floor plan
3 Reflected lobby ceiling plan
4 View of plaza
5 Plaza plan
6 North face of tower
7 Riverside promenade
Photography: Eric Sierins

7

Saigon Centre Project (Phase One)

■ Saigon Centre is an integrated mixed-use development strategically located on Ho Chi Minh City's main thoroughfare, Le Loi Boulevard. Situated in the center of the commercial district, it is within walking distance of major hotels, government offices, commercial establishments, and tourist attractions.

Phase One was to be developed as the most prestigious commercial address in Ho Chi Minh City, incorporating a truly international building that would not readily date. Furthermore, the design was to avoid any colonial pastiche treatment, and local authorities emphasized the need for ease of public access into and through the site as well as stipulating an amount of open public space within the site.

In response to the existing French and American colonial buildings of Ho Chi Minh City, the concept of a constant three-level colonnaded podium was developed for the street edges, with tower setbacks of 10 meters from the main boulevard and 5 meters from the side roads. A promenade through the site leads from a major gateway on Le Loi Boulevard, and an arrival courtyard is a reinterpretation of traditional French colonial planning. Non-uniformity of tower heights in each phase creates diversity and interest on the skyline.

The completed Phase One development is a mixed-use 25-story retail, office, and serviced apartment tower. To reduce the impact of a large floor plate, the tower corners have been eroded, while vertical slots further break down the elevational bulk to accentuate the tower's height. The angled lower floor plate addresses the road junction at the site's corner, and a three-story high entrance serves to make a feature and acts as a focus. The retail accommodation extends from the street to the internal promenade. Spacious walkways link all levels of the podium retail and restaurant areas with the office and residential floors above.

The client expressed the desire for granite to be used for the cladding, but the availability of materials in Vietnam meant that a balance needed to be struck between the conservative appeal of natural stone and the use of metal panels to articulate the elevation. In contrast to the main elevation, the angled lower floors utilize aluminum panels with flush glazing. The perception of quality and the practicality of maintenance requirements were important issues.

Location
Ho Chi Minh City, Vietnam

Completion
1997

Height
106 m

Stories
25

Area
Site: 2,260 m² (phase 1); building: 24,000 m²

Structure
Reinforced concrete

Materials
Aluminum, granite, and glass cladding system

Use
Office, retail, apartments, carparking

Cost
US$45 million

Architect
Denton Corker Marshall Group

Structural engineer
Maunsell Consultants Asia Ltd

Services engineer
Rust JRP Asia Pacific Ltd

Client
First Pacific Straits Land (Saigon) Ltd

Contractor
John Laing International / COFICO JV

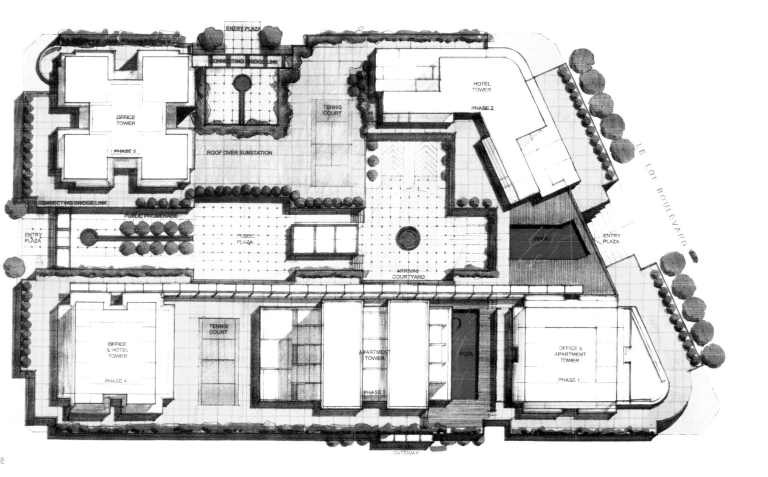

1   View of completed Phase 1 from Le Loi Boulevard
2   Site plan
3   View of model of entire development proposal
Photography: courtesy Denton Corker Marshall Group

Sathorn City Tower

■ The distinctive upward taper of Sathorn City Tower is derived in response to street shadow regulations, and is further enhanced by the large entrance plaza set back from bustling Sathorn Road.

The 32-story volume is divided into various contrasting elements, held together by the powerful symmetry and a common choice of materials including Thai pink granite.

Alternating solid and open elements around the base anchor the six-story carpark podium to the inclined office tower, which culminates in a lighter 'peristyle' roof feature.

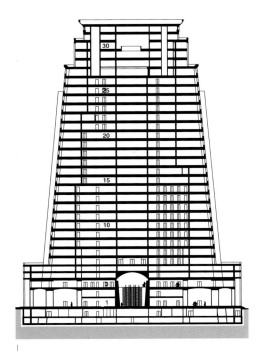

1

2

Location
Bangkok, Thailand

Completion
1994

Height
115.85 m

Stories
32 and 2 basements

Area
Site: 17,180 m²; superstructure: 102,000 m²

Structure
Reinforced concrete

Materials
Thai granite, reflective glass, and aluminum windows

Use
Commercial

Cost
1,450 million Baht

Architect
P&T Group

Structural engineer
Torpong & Associate Co., Ltd

Client
City Realty (Bangkok Bank) Co., Ltd

Contractor
Thai Mazama Co., Ltd

3

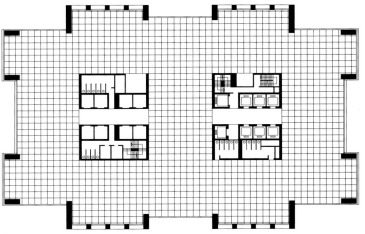

4

6

5

1   *Diagrammatic section*
2   *Exterior*
3   *Spacious main entrance hall*
4   *Typical floor plan*
5   *Ground floor lift lobby*
6   *Spacious main lobby*
Photography: courtesy P&T Group

SEG Plaza

■ The site is in the center of downtown Shenzhen. The plaza provides exhibition space, offices, department stores, commercial information and recreation facilities, and a stock exchange. With a total height of 292 meters, the new building consists of 72 stories above ground, in the podium and the tower, and a four-story underground carpark.

Because the site is at an intersection, it was not possible to place a square in front of it. Instead, the tower is placed at the northeast corner and the podium stretches along the street frontage.

A public square is placed in a three-story half-open space on the first-floor level, leaving maximum floor space for retail at street level. The half-open square provides easy access to the adjacent light rail system, as well as to elevated passageways, escalators, and stairs leading to the offices, shops, and carpark. Provision is also made for future subway access. In this way, vehicles and pedestrians are safely separated.

The tower is octagonal in plan, with an overall column grid of 43.1 x 43.1 meters. Elevators, stairs, sanitary facilities, and other service functions are placed at the center. The structure is a tube of reinforced concrete and represents the tallest building of its type in the world. The façade is a gray glass curtain wall with gold-outlined aluminum panels, giving an appearance of noble simplicity.

The project has a Neo-Classical flavor, providing a unique architectural presence in Shenzhen. The glass curtain wall, belt windows, and colorful bands of the façade give the building a simple, clear, and upright aspect. On the top level a club and bar, a helicopter pad, and satellite antennas add to the building's high-tech appearance.

1

Location
Shenzhen, People's Republic of China

Completion
1999

Height
292 m

Stories
72 and 4 underground

Area
Site: 9,653 m²; floor: 175 m²

Structure
Steel and concrete

Materials
Curtain wall, metal panel, stone

Architect
Hua Yi Designing Consultants Ltd

Client
Seg Plaza Investment & Development Co. Ltd

2

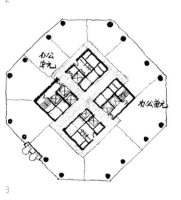

3

1   Tower view from west
2   General view from west
3   Tower floor plan
4   Ground floor plan
Photography: courtesy Hua Yi Designing Consultants Ltd

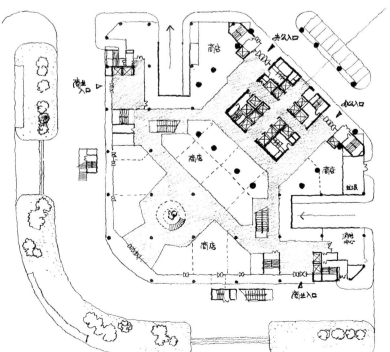

4

Shanghai Centre

■ The Shanghai Centre, a complete business, living and recreation environment, was the first multi-use complex and one of the largest foreign investment projects in China when it opened in 1990. Designed to accommodate the international business traveler in a world that had not been open to the West, Shanghai Centre offered an environment not only sympathetic to the diverse foreign tenant cultures, but also welcoming to the local Chinese people. Rather than attempting to mimic Chinese architecture, the design intent abstracted the forms, images, even gardens traditionally found in China for use in this very modern center.

Reverence towards the context was established as a direct rapport with local culture. The street level plan was generated from a Chinese view of organizing space. The complex is entered by an open gateway, then organizes symmetrically about the north and south axes. Like the plan for the Palace for Happiness in the Forbidden City, the complex's plan elevated each building above the main central court, with stairs leading up to each entrance, and gardens lining the entry court.

In line with the traditional housing orientation, the complex faces south, opening onto Nanjing Road—a street as renowned as the Champs Elysees or Fifth Avenue. At nearly 185,800 square meters, the complex offers a 47-story, 700-room, five-star hotel; two 24-story apartment towers of approximately 500 apartment suites; a prime office and showroom facility; a variety of retail components; a 4,645 square meter exhibition space; a 1000-seat theater; a skylit 15 meter high multi-use atrium; a multifunctional roof garden; health club; parking for 350 cars and an equal number of bicycles; and an entry level courtyard which has drawn wide acclaim for its functional simplicity and its contextual Nanjing Road features.

Shanghai Centre's original and now current mission is to champion the repositioning of the city for new trade in the areas of high-tech, manufacturing, and banking. The design had to create an economic focal point for Shanghai to which neighboring developments could relate. Working with the Chinese government, the architect created the central concept of a 'city-within-a-city' that would respond to the demands of a growing city and the needs of its new business community.

1

2

Location
Shanghai, People's Republic of China

Completion
1989

Height
168 m

Stories
Hotel: 47; residential: 24

Area
Complex: 185,800 m²

Structure
Reinforced concrete

Materials
Concrete frame with a concrete shear wall core

Use
Office, residential, hotel, retail

Cost
US$105 million

Architect
John Portman & Associates

Associate architect
East China Architectural Design and Research Institute

Structural engineer
John Portman & Associates (now AES)

Service engineer
Newcomb & Boyd Engineers

Client
SeaCliff, Ltd

Contractor
Kajima Corporation

3

4

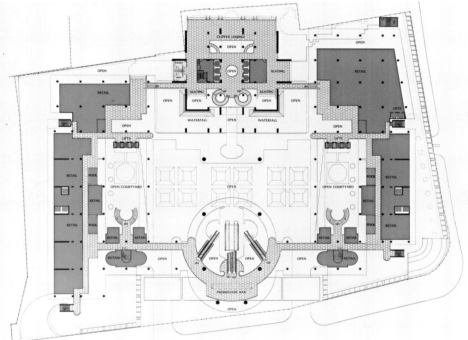

5

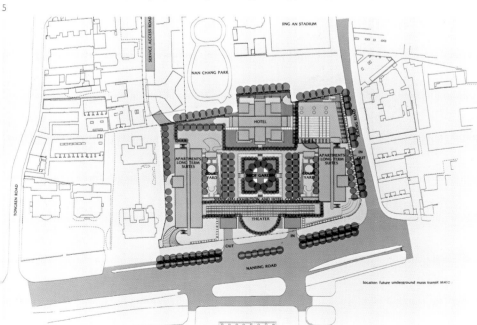

6

7

1&2   Exterior front
3   Lobby lounge
4   Summer pavilion
5   Retail mezzanine (level 2) floor plan
6   Site plan
7   Shanghai Museum

Photography: courtesy Michael Portman/John Portman & Associates (1,2), The Portman Ritz-Carlton, Shanghai (3,4,7)

Shanghai Securities Exchange Building

■ Winner of an international design competition, the Shanghai Securities Exchange Building is a 26-story, widely acclaimed landmark in the Pudong Development area of Shanghai.

The design concept is simple and dramatic and consists of three main compositional elements: the podium, the bridge structure containing the office, and the soaring telecommunications tower, combined to create the building's unique imagery. In keeping with its high-technology orientation, architectural detailing is contemporary and provides rich and elegant façades to the project.

Above the podium, each side of the office bridge form rises independently for 10 floors. The sides then join together and span across the podium to provide an additional eight floors of office space. The dramatic void created beneath the offices is one of the most distinguishing features of the Securities Exchange. Also described as a 'gateway', the form of the building frames the view of a park located in the center of the block.

The soaring antenna is emblematic of the international communications that are so important to the functioning of the Securities Exchange. Approximately 100 meters in total height, some 40 meters of which are above the roof of the building, the antenna establishes a direct connection from the trading floor, through the bridge to the skyline.

The lobby also features artwork by a local artist, telling the history of Chinese money. The dramatic void in the exterior form of the building is reminiscent of the square hole in the center of the traditional Chinese coin— appropriate imagery for a Securities Exchange.

Interior materials restate the high-tech theme and include stainless steel, silver metal, and clear glass panels, accented by polished granite and marble. The limited use of clear-finished maple wood panels complements interior spaces.

A unique, sculptural ceiling using perforated metal panels to create a ceiling wave provides indirect, glare-free lighting to workstations in the main securities hall. Perforated acoustic beechwood panels, combined with solid wood panels are used on perimeter walls throughout. Reception rooms, boardroom, elevators, and elevator lobbies create an elegant and spacious environment for entertaining visiting dignitaries. Lattice work screens are positioned along exterior windows to filter natural light, while providing a decorative backdrop to the rooms.

1

Location
Shanghai, People's Republic of China

Completion
1997

Height
120 m, 180 m to top of antenna

Stories
26 (8-story podium with 34 office floors)

Area
Site: 11,900 m²; building: 95,000 m² (including below-grade area)

Structure
Reinforced concrete, structural steel

Materials
Exterior: glass curtain wall and metal spandrel panels; interior: polished granite, wood, stainless steel, and metal panel accents (lobbies)

Use
Securities Exchange, offices, trading floor facilities, parking

Cost
US$100 million

Architect
WZMH Architects

Associate architect
S A Shanghai Design Institute

Structural engineer
Quinn Dressel & Associates

Mechanical engineer
The Mitchell Partnership

Electrical engineer
Mulvey + Banani International

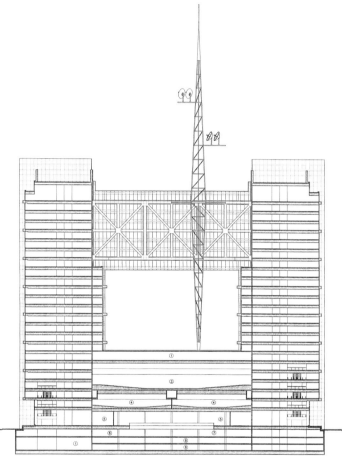

4

Night view
View of main entry lobby
Elevation detail
North-south section
First floor plan
Photography: courtesy WZMH Architects

Client
Shanghai Puly Real Estate Development Company
Contractor
China Construction Company, Team No.8

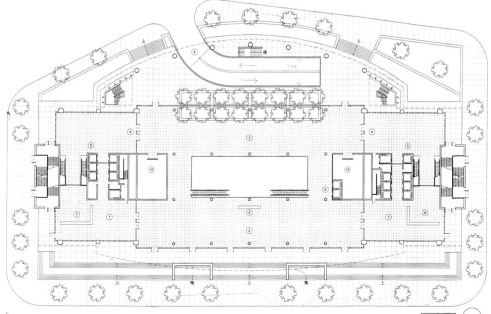

5

0 5 10m

Shenzhen Development Center

■ The Shenzhen Development Center is a modern and comprehensive skyscraper up to international standards. It is located in the heart of the downtown area, adjacent to Shenzhen International Trade Center and the International Commerce Mansion, and not far from the railway station and the Luohu Customs.

The site enjoys exceptional advantages in environment and to one side, the skyscraper has a beautiful view overlooking a street garden. The designing concept stems from the saying 'round heaven and square earth'. The main building is a 43-story cylindrical structure and its podium is a square nine-story building, both of which are steel structures. The 165.3 meter high tower main building is a first-class office. Its lower seven floors connect with the supporting structure to become an entire podium construction, where there are various luxury shops, restaurants, bars, and coffeehouses. The sixth floor and the area below the supporting building are designed to be garages. There is an outdoor swimming pool and a tennis court on the roof of the podium. There is also a helicopter parking area on the roof of the main building.

The shape of the project resembles one terse, tall, and straight pillar supporting the sky. The balconies on the different floors were designed as spiral ladders, creating the sense that the building is rising slowly and gradually, and also a sense that it is moving upwards and is full of vitality. The glass and honeycomb lead-sheet curtain wall was produced by French CFEM Company. The silvery-white appearance and high-tech work make the building look like an exquisite sculpture of modern style against the green plants—shining and sparkling in the sunlight.

1

Location
Shenzhen, People's Republic of China

Completion
1992

Height
165.3 m

Stories
43 and 1 underground

Area
Building: 75,889 m²; site: 7,585m²

Structure
Steel

Materials
Interior: stone, mirror glass, carpet; exterior: curtain wall, aluminum panel

Use
Office complex

Cost
HK$866 million

Architect
Shiyaxi Co. America, Architecture Design Institute Ministry of Construction

Design architect
Dr Owl–CRSS Joint Venture

Client
Shenzhen Development Center Co. Ltd

Contractor
1ˢᵗ Construction company of 3ʳᵈ Bureau of CSCEC

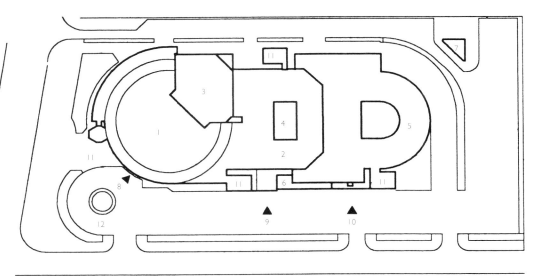

1 Block A high-rise
2 Block B low-rise
3 Helidrome
4 Swimming pool
5 Cooling tower
6 Transformer room
7 Underground gas storage
8 Hotel entrance
9 Office entrance
10 Carpark entrance/exit
11 Stairs
12 Flower pond

0   5   10m   N

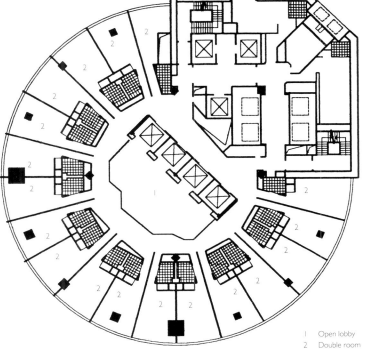

1   Front view
2   Site plan
3   Atrium
4   Entrance
5   Typical floor plan

*Photography: courtesy Architecture Design Institute Ministry
of Construction*

1   Open lobby
2   Double room

Shenzhen Minghua Maritime Center

■ Located at the foot of Guishan Hill in Shekou, Shenzhen, and facing the sea with a hill behind it, Minghua Maritime Center occupies a commanding position with favorable natural terrain. The project consists of an office building and an apartment building, which are joined by a podium.

In the general layout plan, the view of scenic spots was the top priority. Based on the various functional requirements and the owners' needs, and considering the overall arrangement of existing buildings and natural topographical features, the project was divided with other buildings, squares, roads, and planted areas into different functional spaces. The newly built office building joins the apartment building at a right angle. In front of the podium of the office building, a group of high and low squares were arranged in picturesque disorder to separate the traffic system in grade. This arrangement does not impede the view of the earlier-built Minghua Ship Crews Center, and enables various parts of the center to face the sea while avoiding the traffic of people and vehicles.

These buildings operate with the Minghua Ship Crews Center to facilitate services including office, training, hotel and apartment accommodation, restaurant, beverages, and entertainment. Therefore, the architectural modeling was designed to be in concert with the existing buildings as much as possible and, at the same time, to display the features of the project. There is a sightseeing lift specially installed for viewing the landscape from the lobby all the way to the twenty-forth floor. There is also a roof garden on the podium.

1

Location
Shenzhen, People's Republic of China

Completion
1996

Height
100 m

Stories
24 and 2 underground

Area
Building: 73,000 m²; site: 16,000 m²

Structure
Frame shear wall

Materials
Interior: hollow block; exterior: aluminum panel, tile, stone

Use
Apartments, offices

Cost
460 million RMB

Architect
Architecture Design Institute Ministry of Construction

Client
Minghua Shipping Co. Ltd

Contractor
Construction Bureau of Ministry of Railways

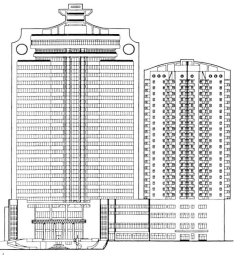

1	Minghua Maritime Center	5	Flower pond
2	Minghua Phase I project	6	Fountain
3	Bike shed	7	Carpark
4	Cooling tower	8	Flag pole

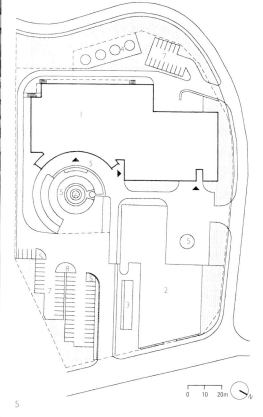

0   10   20m   N

5

1   Front view
2   Part view
3   Entrance
4   Elevation
5   Site plan
Photography: courtesy Architecture Design Institute Ministry of
Construction

Shenzhen Units Plaza

■ Shengzhen Units Plaza is located in the Futian District of Shenzhen. As a large public skyscraper with a height of 195 meters, it is used as commercial offices and accommodation for ministries and commissions under the state council, as well as enterprises under the control of the provinces and municipalities in Shenzhen to strengthen technical cooperation and trade ties with Shenzhen.

The building is composed of four parts: an apartment office building, an office building, a guesthouse, and a department store with accesses and elevators respectively. There are 30 high-speed elevators and 20 escalators in the building, and a parking lot with a capacity for 462 cars. The internal traffic within the site has been arranged in an efficient and convenient way.

The design has made the high-rise main building and auxiliary buildings into a complex. The main building, which is in the shape of a windmill, and the auxiliary buildings, which stand at both sides in two bending rows, form an inner courtyard of 30 meters in diameter in between, implying unity and cooperation. Such a plan makes the elevation modeling magnificent and perfect, integrative and vivacious. The windmill-shaped main building implies a steady climb, symbolizing the ascendant situation of Shenzhen's special economic zone in its second flourish, and the magnificent and prosperous image of this modernized city.

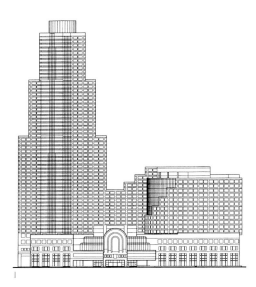

1

2

Location
Shenzhen, People's Republic of China

Completion
1998

Height
195 m

Stories
56 and 3 underground

Area
Building: 215,600 m²; site: 18,000 m²

Structure
Frame shear wall

Materials
Interior: lightweight block; exterior: aluminum pane, tile, stone

Use
Offices, hotel, commercial

Cost
1.185 billion RMB

Architect
Architecture Design Institute Ministry of Construction

Client
Shenzhen Economic Coordination Development Co.

Contractor
3rd Huaxi Construction Company

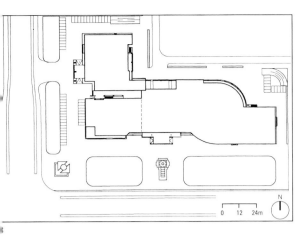

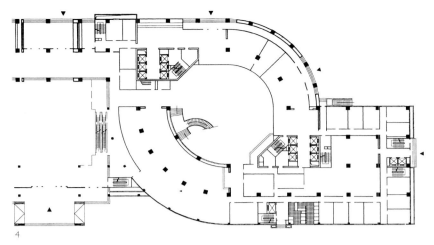

1   Elevation
2   Whole view
3   Site plan
4   Block B plan
5   Main entrance
Photography: courtesy of Architecture Design Institute Ministry
of Construction

Shin-Yokohama
Prince Hotel

■ Shin-Yokohama Prince Hotel was planned to be part of core facilities that include a large retail building in the newly developed Shin-Yokohama area of Yokohama city, which was established as the port when Japan opened to foreign countries about 140 years ago.

The hotel is comprised of 1,002 guestrooms, 23 banquet rooms, and 11 restaurants and bars. The design and engineering theme is 'towards the future'—appropriate to the challenging facility and area. A cylinder-shape was adopted, finished in glass and aluminum panels to express a futuristic image. There were many engineering challenges, and new technologies were used to realize the building.

The tower had to be structurally engineered to tolerate winds and earthquakes. A double-tube structure was used, which has a doughnut-shape plan—the first in the world—and which supports the 42-story, 149.35 meter high futuristic cylinder tower.

Another challenge was the sway caused by the wind. A device harnessing water was installed at the top of the tower, which decreases 50 percent of the shake.

The influence of the wind was carefully investigated; it was realized that the huge force occurring on the surface due to the wind did not separate smoothly from the cylinder. Thus an exterior aluminum panel embossed with a half-cocoon shape was employed, which reduces 30 percent of the wind force.

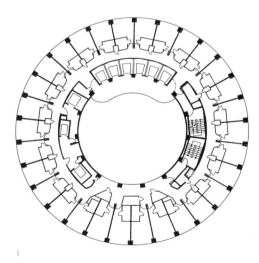

1

2

Location
Yokohama City, Japan

Completion
March 1992

Height
149.35 m

Stories
42

Area
Building: 127,194.49 m²

Materials
Tower: aluminum cast panel and glass; basement: ceramic tiled precast concrete panel; interior: marble, painted gypsum board

Use
Hotel

Architect
Design Department, Shimizu Corporation

Structural engineer
Design Department, Shimizu Corporation

Service engineer
Design Department, Shimizu Corporation

Client
SEIBU RAILWAY Co. Ltd

Contractor
Shimizu Corporation

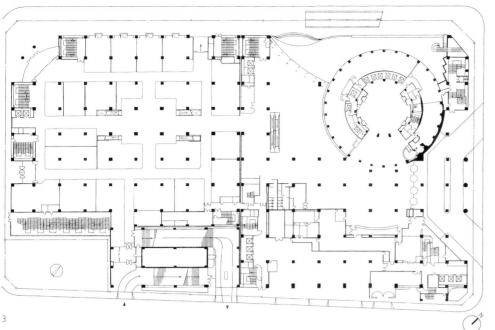

3

4

5

1 Typical floor plan
2 View from ground
3 Ground floor plan
4 Atrium
5 Bar
Photography: Shinkenchiku-Sha

Shinagawa Intercity

■ Shinagawa Station is the southern entrance to the city of Tokyo. The project site used to be a part of the old cargo yard of the station. A total area of about 16.2 hectares was designated by city planning as a redevelopment area. The master plan for the area takes up about 10 hectares, and on this is placed a series of parks called Pedestrian Valley (40–60 meters wide and 400 meters long). This valley connects the buildings on both sides: on one side, Shinagawa Intercity, and on the other side, several more buildings are planned and will be built soon.

Intercity has a total floor area of over 300,000 square meters, and the total height is limited by aviation control of Haneda Airport. Under these conditions, there was an attempt to not create a massive and oppressive wall, so space was left between Tower A and Tower B and C to let the air and sunshine come through.

A wide pedestrian deck on the second floor level with a large and long roof was designed. This deck, called Skyway, was laid along the Pedestrian Valley. Skyway, as the axis, penetrates through Intercity and weaves the atrium, galleria, and lobbies of each building, and connects offices, shops, restaurants, and the cultural hall together.

The glazing of the tower buildings was developed specially for this project; high transparency with high heat reflectiveness. This softens the overwhelming mass of the buildings and shows what is inside to welcome visitors. Also, there was an attempt to use glass as much as possible to maintain transparency and to not block out the visibility of the facilities.

After a few years, when Pedestrian Valley is completed, the basement level of the Intercity will face the valley on the same level, which will enlarge the exposure of the lower portion of the buildings to the open space.

1

Location
Tokyo, Japan

Completion
November 1998

Height
Tower A: 144.5 m; Tower B: 139.9 m;
Tower C: 139.9 m

Stories
32 and 1 basement

Area
Floor: 343,100 m²

Materials
Aluminum curtain wall with transparent reflective glass, aluminum panel with baked paint, porcelain tile

Use
Office, retail, and auditorium

Cost
¥128.000 million

Architect
Nihon Sekkei Inc.

Executive architect
Toru Aragane

Structural engineer
Nihon Sekkei Inc.

Owner/Client
Kowa Real Estate Development Co. Ltd, Minato Urban Development Co. Ltd, Obayashi Corporation

Contractor
Obayashi Corporation

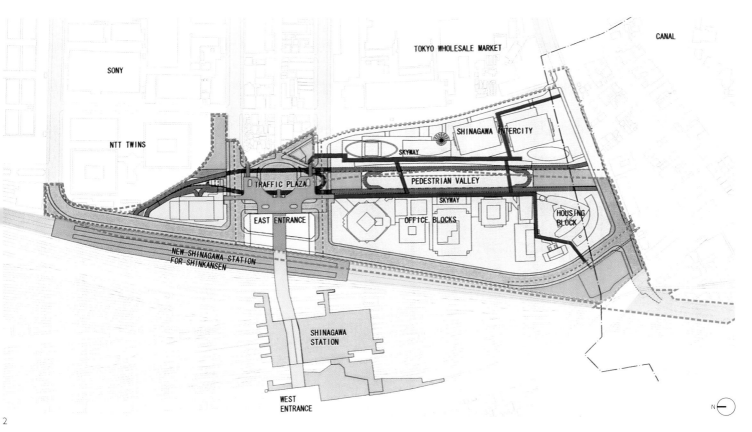

TOKYO WHOLESALE MARKET

CANAL

SONY

NTT TWINS

SHINAGAWA INTERCITY

SKYWAY

TRAFFIC PLAZA

PEDESTRIAN VALLEY

EAST ENTRANCE

OFFICE BLOCKS

SKYWAY

HOUSING BLOCK

NEW SHINAGAWA STATION FOR SHINKANSEN

SHINAGAWA STATION

WEST ENTRANCE

N

2

3

4

1   East-side view
2   Site plan
3   Shinagawa Intercity seen from Shinagawa Station
4   Skyway and atrium
Photography: Kawasumi Architectural Photography, Nihon Sekkei Inc.

Shinjuku Park Tower

■ Built in the southwest corner of the Shinjuku New Center area, this complex of offices, hotel, and showrooms serves as the terminus of an axis created by the long, narrow Chuo Public Park running north-south. This axis determined the building's orientation and the characteristic configuration of Tokyo's skyline. This multipurpose building complex with its high-rise tower can also be seen as an extension of Chuo Park, with a large portion of the site carefully landscaped. An atrium inside further enhances the lush green atmosphere.

This building, rising to a height of 233 meters, consists of 52 floors above ground and five floors below. The overall great mass of the building has been articulated as a configuration of three diminishing towers to minimize its impact on the surrounding area and reduce the shadow over the park. It also made a gesture to preserve the continuity with the surrounding business district by matching the orientation of the city hall complex nearby.

This mixed-use building encloses 263,836 square meters and accommodates a luxury hotel with 178 rooms. Arriving guests are greeted with a breathtaking view of the city as they ride the shuttle elevator connecting the hotel's second floor entrance hall with the forty-first floor sky lobby. The view from the top floor hotel rooms is equally spectacular.

Below the hotel are 30 floors of office space. With its 2.7 meter high ceilings and a raised access panel floor system, an unconstrained working space was created that would be very responsive to various needs of the tenants. The lower levels of the building contain a series of showrooms known as the 'Ozone', serving as a multipurpose design center.

Tokyo Gas Shinjuku District Heating and Cooling Center maintains a heating and cooling plant on the basement level, and showrooms on the first and second levels. The atrium connects the various parts of the building to the Shinjuku Central Heating Station.

Location
Tokyo, Japan

Completion
1994

Height
233 m

Stories
52

Area
Building: 263,836 m²

Structure
Steel

Use
Mixed use

Architect
Kenzo Tange Associates

Structural engineer
Kobori Research Complex, Inc.

Service engineer
Inuzuka Engineering Consultants

Developer
Tokyo Gas Urban Project

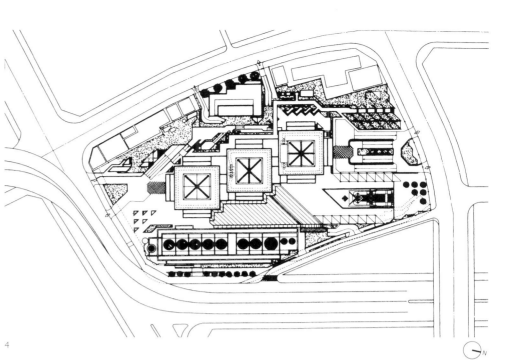

5

1 Appearing like three distinct towers, Shinjuku Park Tower is
  actually one
2 Entrance
3 Girandole
4 Site plan
5 The Peak Lounge
6 Park Hyatt room
Photography: Osamu Murai courtesy Park Hyatt Tokyo

6

Sinn Sathorn Tower

■ Sinn Sathorn Tower is a 43-floor tower. It is located by the Chao Praya River, which is not far from the central business district of Bangkok. The main road in front of the building is connected to Sathorn Road, which is the old household area of Bangkok. For the podium section of the building, the façade was designed to correspond with these old household buildings. The tower section, which is the office space, is designed as an 'intelligent building'. The building design is a prominent landmark in this area of Bangkok.

1

2

Location
Bangkok, Thailand

Completion
April 1993

Height
195 m including antenna

Stories
43

Area
100,000 m²

Structure
Cast-in-place concrete

Materials
Exterior: flurocarbon paint on prefabricated concrete; aluminum-frame windows

Use
Offices

Cost
800 million Baht

Architect
Plan Architect Co., Ltd; Plan Associates Co., Ltd; Plan Studio Co., Ltd

Associate architect
Arun Chaiseri Consulting Engineers Co., Ltd

System engineer
SEM Engineering Co., Ltd

Construction management
South East Asia Technology Co., Ltd

Client
Thanasathorn Corp., Ltd

Cont ractor
Siam Syntech Co., Ltd

3

4

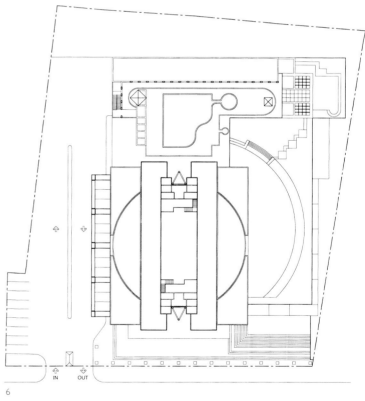

6

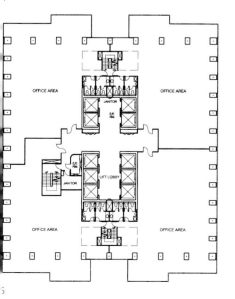

5

1 Front entrance
2 View from west towards Bangkok side
3 Looking up at tower
4 Entrance foyer
5 Floor plan (levels 12–41)
6 Site plan
Photography: Mr Piphat Phattanathavorn

St Luke's Garden

■ St Luke's Garden is composed of care residences, a sports club, and a hotel, which are part of the very conception of the life science center aimed at by St Luke's International Hospital, as well as tenant offices that are the main financial source for the entire redevelopment.

The basic design policy for St Luke's garden, which is a multipurpose facility, was to plan the office tower and the residential tower not as isolated independent towers, but as 'twin towers' communicating with each other.

Both twin towers, which are given delicate complexions by corner-cut and setback, create appearances with something in common. Also, the atrium at the base (large roof plaza) and the high aerial bridge connecting the two buildings generate a characteristic silhouette involving the twin high-rise towers communicating to each other.

The bridge, which characterizes the whole appearance, connects the elevator transfer level of the office building with the lounge/restaurant level of the hotel building so that the hotel can be reached directly from the office building without once going down to the ground level. This bridge is located approximately 110 meters above ground, so it requires high expansion/contraction performance. It is designed as a steel truss tube structure, with one end pin-fixed and the other having pin rollers placed on 4 meter rails.

The second levels of the buildings have ground foundations that gradually lower from the large roof plaza, to the outside plaza, to the hydrophilic park on the embankment, and finally to the waterside terrace to create a space that appears to be melting into the surrounds.

The glass screen of the large roof plaza is constructed by the dot-point method for high transparency to enhance the integration of the atrium interior with the Sumida River. Further, the roof glass is structure-sealed to maintain the lightness of the glass as seen from the river.

1

Location
Tokyo, Japan

Completion
May 1994

Height
220.63 m

Stories
Office: 51 and 4 underground; residential: 38 and 4 underground

Area
Site: 13,033 m²; building: 9,291 m²;
total floor: 170,781 m²

Structure
Offices: steel; residential: steel reinforced concrete

Use
Offices, residential, athletic club, restaurants, shops medical clinic, security center, hotel

Architect
Nikken Sekkei Ltd

Associate architect
Tokyu Architects & Engineers Inc.

Client
Mitsui Real Estate Development Co., Nippon Life Insurance Co., Tokyo Land Corp., Matsushita Investment and Development Co. Ltd, Towa Real Estate

Contractor
Kajima Corporation, Taisei Corporation, Obayashi Corporation, Shimuzu Corporation, Maeda Corporation

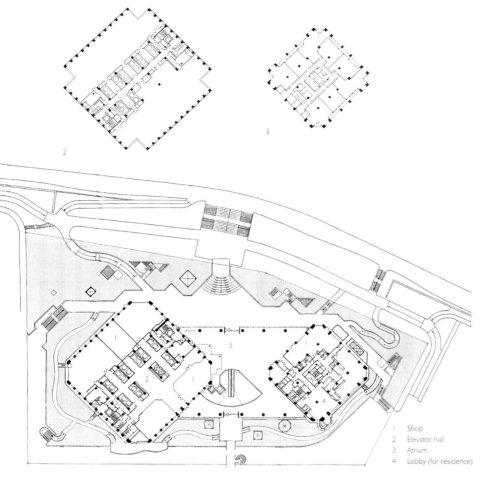

2

3

4

1	Shop
2	Elevator hall
3	Atrium
4	Lobby (for residence)

5

6

1 Elevation
2 Typical floor plan (office)
3 Typical floor plan (residence)
4 Second floor plan
5 Atrium
6 Sky restaurant
Photography: Hiroshi Shinozawa

Suzhou Industrial Park International Tower

■ Suzhou Industrial Park is a new town of 70 square kilometers financed by a joint venture between the government of the People's Republic of China and the government of Singapore. The objective of the development is to establish and maintain a very high international level of quality in all aspects: selection of tenants, quality of construction, maintenance, and operation. The industrial park consists of light industrial developments on the perimeter and a commercial core district in the center. The commercial core district provides the industrial park with modern offices, single and multi-family housing, a shopping center, cinemas, restaurants, and other entertainment facilities.

Lohan Associates was selected to design the Suzhou Industrial Park International Tower (SIPIT) for the Industrial Park Administrative Committee as a result of an international design competition. SIPIT will house the administrative committee offices for the new industrial park, as well as public cultural facilities.

The competition called for the design of a 'city hall'—a physical and symbolic center for the new Suzhou Industrial Park. As the first office building to be constructed in the commercial core district, it is to embody the future aspiration of the industrial park. The goal was to provide an efficient and effective environment within which the business of the industrial park is conducted, and to establish a standard level of design and construction quality to be emulated by future buildings in the park.

The 56,000 square meter multi-use building consists of two floors of basement, six floors of podium and 12 floors of office space. The podium includes conference facilities, council chambers, library, exhibitions, and restaurants.

The basic mass of the building is made of two types of forms. The center elliptical low-e glass curtain wall element is held in place by rectilinear granite-clad solid elements. The whole building is designed around a five-story tall open atrium space. The atrium space, which is under the tower and between the two wings of the podium, is the connecting link between the outdoor spaces to the north and south, and in another area it links the east and west wings of the podium to the high-rise tower above.

Architecture reflects the values and objectives of the people it services. With this building, it is hoped that this development process will result in a dynamic metropolis that balances government, public spaces, and nature in true harmony.

1

Location
Suzhou, People's Republic of China

Completion
December 1999

Height
88 m

Stories
18

Area
56,000 m²

Structure
Reinforced concrete

Materials
Granite and aluminum curtain wall

Use
Government offices

Cost
US$50 million

Architect
Lohan Associates, Inc.

Associate architect
Suzhou Industrial Park Design & Research Institute

Structural engineer
Suzhou Industrial Park Design & Research Institute

Service engineer
Fred Huang & Associates, William Yang & Associates

Interior designer
IA Interior Architect, Inc.

Client
China-Singapore Suzhou Industrial Park Administrative Committee

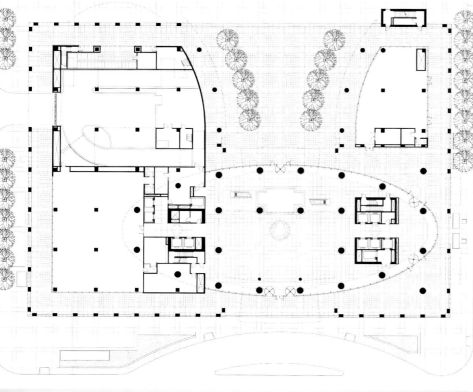

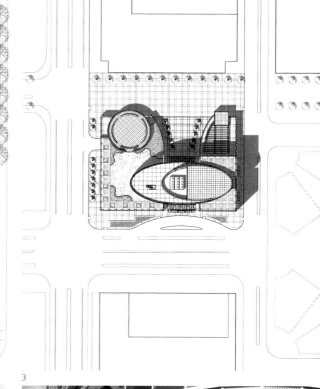

3

5

1   Suzhou Industrial Park International Tower
2   Ground floor plan
3   Site plan
4   Plaza entry
5   Exterior façade
Photography: courtesy Lohan Associates, Inc., Doug Snower (4)

T&C Tower

■ From the moment of its inception, the 85-floor T&C Tower was to be a Taiwanese landmark with a strong traditional Chinese flavor.

The base of this high-rise is raised higher than other similar buildings to make way for a tunnel underneath. This architecture considers the weather, typography, and aesthetics, in addition to meeting the ancient Chinese principles of geometry.

Internally the building is constructed around eight different cores; this allows easy access to and through the building's accommodation, including lounges, shipping areas, and office space. Each of these areas is also independent, each with their own gateway extending towards the sky lobby. The building gains its basic structure vertically from the eight elevator shafts and horizontally from the mechanical floor. The overall spatial structure is created by piling a pagoda-style tower atop two lofty podiums. The core of the three units is designed as a high atrium, which facilitates sunlight illumination, creates a vivid space, and allows separate office units to communicate with one another. Moreover, by reducing the wind pressure, this massive void in the center also serves a crucial structural function.

1

2

Location
Kaohsiung, Taiwan

Completion
August 1998

Height
348 m

Stories
85 and 5 basements

Area
Site: 12,006 m²; floor: 306, 337 m²

Structure
Steel and concrete

Materials
Granite

Use
Mixed use, including department store, hotel, amusement center, serviced apartments

Architect
C.Y. Lee & Partners, Architects & Planners

Associate architect
HOK Architects

Structural engineer
Evergreen Engineers

Mechanical/Electrical engineer
CEC

Client
Tuntex & Chien Tai Group

Contractor
Tuntex

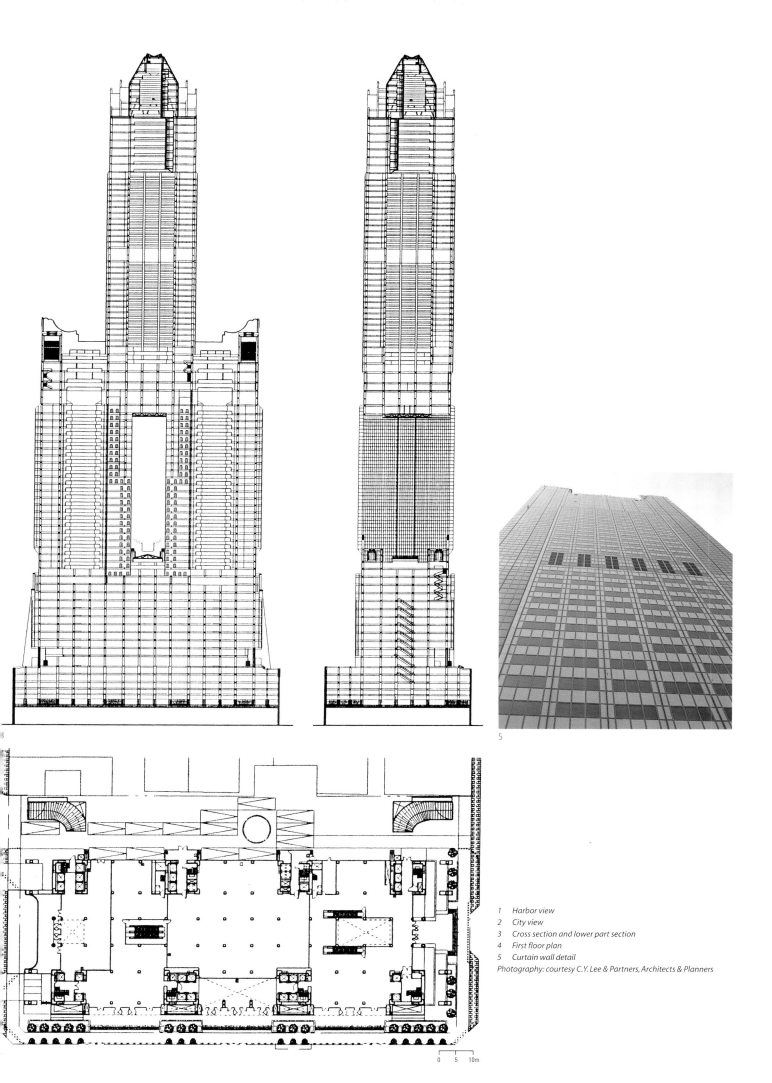

1   Harbor view
2   City view
3   Cross section and lower part section
4   First floor plan
5   Curtain wall detail
Photography: courtesy C.Y. Lee & Partners, Architects & Planners

0   5   10m

Taipei Metro

■ This large mixed-use commercial complex was constructed at Tung Hwa South Road, one of the attractive, tree-lined boulevards in the centre of Taipei. The essentially rectangular site permitted a total building area of 110,000 square meters, with the client's brief calling for a headquarter office building, a five-star hotel, retail, and associated carparking and services.

The design translated this into a development consisting of two 42-story towers, which rise above a six-story podium and six basement levels. The office tower contains first-class office accommodation for the Far Eastern Group on 32 floors, including the executive floors at the upper levels. The second tower, a twin in size and form to the office tower, contains the deluxe Taipei Shangri-La Hotel.

The hotel public areas and the related back-of-house facilities occupy the podium structure and parts of the basement levels.

A circular, multi-story high entrance foyer forms the focal point of the hotel and overlooks the entrance forecourt and fountain. The 420 luxuriously appointed guestrooms are housed in the tower, topped by restaurants and recreation facilities.

The mall, an exclusive retail complex occupied by Joyce, extends over all of the podium levels. It is focused around an attractive, skylit atrium space, created on the main axis in between the two towers. A cone-shaped skylight crowns the atrium.

Trees, escalators, and lifts in exciting configurations combined with water features have been introduced, enticing tenants and visitors alike to explore, shop, and enjoy themselves.

The hotel and retail complex and the office tower have their own, separate entry points. The granite-paved plaza or forecourt at the base of the two towers acts as the formal driveway to the office tower.

Typhoon conditions equal to Hong Kong combined with Taiwan's seismic conditions were a major consideration to the configuration of the two high-rise towers. The project is clad in aluminum panels with flush set windows in combination with an all-glass curtain wall, applied to all-curved elements of the project.

The podium or base is lined with matching polished Brazilian Granite, in combination with Dakota Mahogany Granite and polished stainless accents.

1

Location
Taipei, Taiwan

Completion
December 1994

Height
165 m

Stories
42

Area
Site: 10,000 m²; superstructure: 160,000 m²

Structure
Structural steel

Materials
Aluminum, reflective glass, and Brazilian and US granites

Use
Commercial, hotel, retail

Cost
US$325 million

Architect
P&T Group

Associate architect
C.Y. Lee & Partners, Architects & Planners

Structural engineer
T.Y. Lin International

Service engineer (M&E)
William Tao & Associates / I.S. Lin & Associates

Client
Far Eastern Textile Ltd; Asia Cement Corp.; Yuan Dong Construction Co., Ltd

Contractor
Da Cin Contractor Co., Ltd

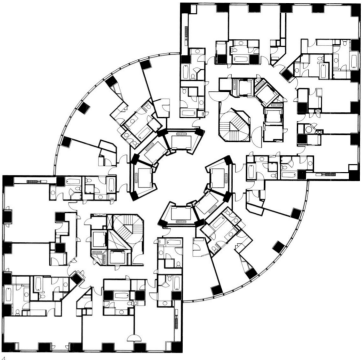

4

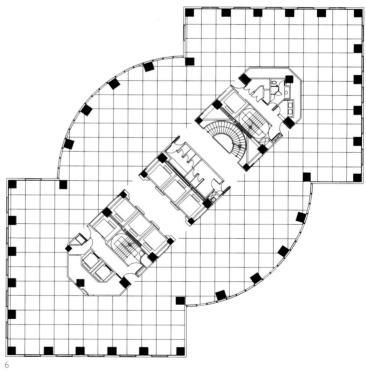

6

1   View from Tung-Hwa South Road
2   Exterior
3   Main lobby of hotel
4   Floor plan (hotel)
5   Executive floor skylight entrance lobby with 'Chu Ming' sculpture
6   Floor plan (office)
Photography: courtesy P&T Group

Thai Wah Tower II

■ The 60-story Thai Wah Tower II, linked to the smaller and older Tower I, is located on Sathorn Road, in the heart of Bangkok's business and embassy district. It contains offices for sale or rental; the five-star Westin Banyan Tree Hotel; the Banyan Tree Spa and Skydeck; a club with lounge and fine-dining restaurant; and supporting facilities.

Due to a tight site, these components do not occupy separate buildings but are placed on top of each other; thus the circulation of office workers, hotel guests, staff, and services had to be segregated carefully by assigning different entry levels and separate lift systems.

The tower is very slim because of zoning laws. To stiffen it, the architect placed a lift core at each end, plus one in the middle, like a tripod. The exterior is clad in mirror-glass but the three lift cores are boldly expressed.

The hotel 'porte-cochere' and lobby are on ground level, overlooking a waterfall garden. Lifts bypass the office floors and go directly to the hotel suites (thirty-third floor and above).

The office 'porte-cochere' is internal (second floor) and leads to the central lifts, which serve the office floors (twelth to thirty-second) but also go down to the basement, where a passage and escalator bring the office workers through Tower I—thus bypassing the hotel 'porte-cochere', and avoiding congestion.

With the spa and Skydeck, the architect could not resist punching a four-story hole right through this thin building. This became the Skydeck (fifty-first to fifty-forth floors) with swimming pool, jacuzzis, lounging deck, and a live Banyan tree. From here, one has a spectacular front-and-back panorama of the city skyline. To left of the Skydeck is the Banyan Tree Spa, with treatment rooms, lockers, and gym; to the right are mechanical services.

Interestingly, the wind-tunnel tests showed that the Skydeck—by letting air blow through—reduces the wind load considerably and allowed the engineer to reduce lateral stiffening.

Since its completion, Thai Wah Tower II has become a bold addition to the Bangkok skyline. Reflecting the owner's wishes, the architect strived for simple dignity and clean, timeless proportions, independent of prevailing architectural fashions.

1

Location
Bangkok, Thailand

Completion
Office: January 1995; hotel: August 1996

Height
194 m from ground level to roof parapet

Stories
60 (excluding basement)

Area
57,000 m²

Structure
Reinforced concrete

Materials
External: mirror glass cladding; concrete with textured paint and grooves

Use
Hotel, spa, offices

Cost
2,000 million Baht

Architect
Architrave Design & Planning Co. Ltd

Owner
Thai Wah Plaza Ltd

Structural engineer
Arun Chaiseri Consulting Engineers Co. Ltd

Mechanical and electrical engineer
Southeast Asia Technology Co. Ltd

Wind tunnel study
Department of Civil Engineering, National University of Singapore

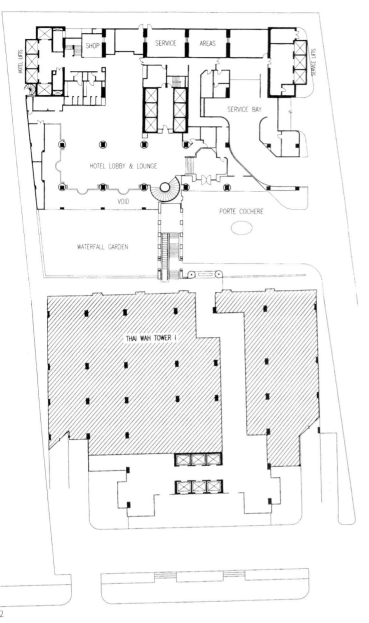

Interior designer
HL Lim & Associates Private Limited

Main contractor
Philipp Holzmann (Thai) Ltd

Site supervision
Southeast Asia Technology Co. Ltd

Construction management
Thai Wah Engineering Co. Ltd

1   View from below
2   Site plan
3   View from across Sathorn Road, with the 24-story Thai Wah Tower I in front, and the 60-story Tower II behind
4   Skydeck, with pool and jacuzzi in the foreground and Bangkok skyline in the rear
5   Bai Yun (Chinese restaurant) on sixtieth floor, with curved vault above

Photography: courtesy Architrave Design & Planning Co. Ltd and Westin Banyan Tree Hotel

Times Square

■ Times Square is located on the former Tram Depot site that is over 10,000 square meters in area. It has a gross floor area of over 180,000 square meters plus four carparking floors. It comprises of two office towers, one 33 stories and the other 26 stories above a 14-story retail podium with four cinemas and a six-story basement. Only 60 percent of the site is built upon, which creates a welcome open space in a highly congested area in Causeway Bay. This open space is now one of the designated locations for New Year's Eve countdown activities, like Times Square in New York.

The MTR Causeway Bay South concourse and its auxiliary spaces in the fifth basement floor links Times Square to the existing MTR Causeway Bay platforms through the tunnels underneath Percival Street.

1

2

Location
Hong Kong SAR, People's Republic of China

Completion
1993

Height
39-story: 202 m; 46-story: 227 m (including basement)

Stories
One 39 and other 46; podium: 14; basements: 6

Area
Building: 180,000 m²; site: 10,400 m²

Structure
Reinforced concrete with structural beams and columns

Materials
Exterior: curtain walling and granite cladding; interior: granite

Use
Commercial, retail

Cost
HK$2,000 million

Architect
Wong & Ouyang (HK) Ltd

Civil and structural engineer
Wong & Ouyang (Civil-Structural Engineering) Ltd

Electrical and mechanical engineer
Wong & Ouyang (Building Services) Ltd

Client
Wharf Properties Ltd

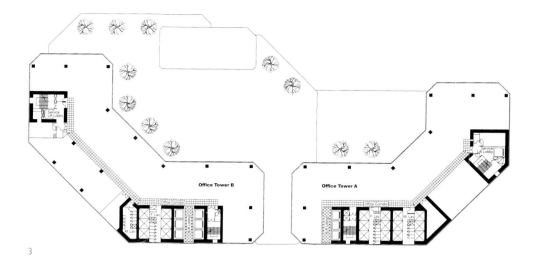

3

4

5

Curtain wall
Heitmann & Associates Inc.

Lighting
Liubeck & Rausch (HK)

Landscape
Team 73

Contractor
Hip Hing Construction Ltd

1   *Mall entrance*
2   *Exterior view*
3   *Typical floor plan*
4&5   *Mall atrium*

Photography: courtesy Wong & Ouyang (HK) Ltd

Tokio Marine Plaza

■ The main theme of the Tokio Marine Plaza is the drama of light and shade created by pure, abstract grids. Although the grids contain structural members that enable 21 x 10.8 meter column-free spaces on the office floors and a tall open space at the foot of the building, they are clad in dark gray-coated aluminum panels whose texture and details are intended to conceal their structural role, neutralize their 'materiality' and thus enhance their abstract quality. The layering of the grids, together with the reflective glass, further intensifies the drama and its complexity.

This structure was developed under the requirement to secure maximum column-free space against seismic movement, but resulted in highly geometrical abstract aesthetics. It can be said that the design is an attempt to break out of the popular banal box-type skyscrapers while pursuing the modernist tradition of abstraction. The abstract grids of the building may bring to one's mind an image of a traditional Japanese building characterized by its beautiful contrast of white walls with posts and beams—whose structural expression has been highly abstracted to suggest only its essence. And one may experience a spatial drama that is similar to those found at the Kiyomizu temple in Kyoto, or the great Buddha hall at the Todai shrine in Nara, Japan. Both are historical masterpieces of traditional Japanese architecture famous for exposed large-scale wooden post and beam structures. This skyscraper could be the first one to reflect the cultural heritage of Japanese traditional architecture.

1

2

Location
Osaka, Japan

Completion
November 1990

Height
118.30 m

Stories
27, 3 basements, and 3 penthouses

Area
Floor area: 68,837.72 m²; site area: 10,721.15 m²

Structure
Steel and reinforced concrete

Materials
Major exterior finishes: 4 mm aluminum panel, fluorocarbon baked finish, pressure equalization curtain wall

Use
Offices and retail

Architect
Kajima Corporation A&E Design Group; Kunihide Oshinomi

Associate architect
Yukishige Miyamae

Mechanical and electrical engineer
Akira Okamoto

Structural engineer
Shigeru Ban

Lighting design
Motoko Ishii

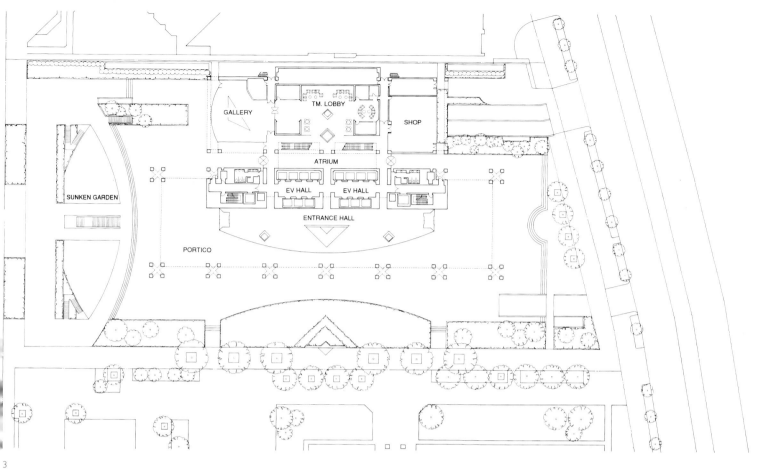

3

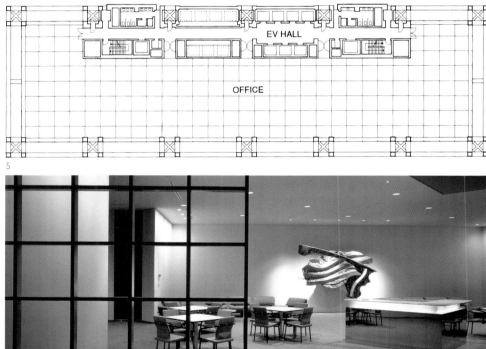

4

5

6

Interior designer
ILYA

Client
The Tokio Marine and Fire Insurance Co., Ltd

Contractor
Kajima Corporation

1   View from Osaka Castle
2   View of external grid
3   Ground floor plan
4   View of entrance hall
5   Typical floor plan
6   View of lobby
Photography: Kiyohiko Higashide (1,2,4), Nacasa & Partners Inc. (6)

Tokyo Opera City Building

■ Tokyo Opera City Building was completed as a private-sector redevelopment project in an existing built-up area surrounding the New National Theater in Tokyo, whose construction was then underway.

The project consists of two major components: a 54-story high-rise tower accommodating approximately 2,000 square meters of office area on each floor, and a low-rise podium block that houses a 1,632-seat concert hall, an art gallery dedicated to contemporary fine art, ICC or NTT Intercommunication Center, which is a museum featuring full utilization of electronics information media, and various commercial facilities.

The podium block also has abundant public spaces, including a 200 meter long barrel-vaulted semi-outdoor galleria; a sunken garden as an outdoor plaza; promenades, and so on.

The exterior walls are composed of granite-clad curtain walls called 'DEWS' (Dry-joint External Wall System).

1

2

Location
Tokyo, Japan

Completion
March 1999

Height
234.371 m

Stories
54, 4 basements, and 2 penthouses

Area
Site: 44,092 m²; built-up area: 13,936 m²; floor: 241,996 m²

Structure
Steel structure, steel and reinforced-concrete composite structure, and reinforced concrete

Use
Offices, commercial, and cultural facilities

Architect
NTT Facilities Inc. Urban Planning & Design Institute Co., TAK Associated Architects Inc.

Developers
Nippon Life Insurance Company; NTT Urban Development Co. Ltd.; Odakyu Department Store Co., Ltd; Keio Electric Railway Co., Ltd; The Dai-ichi Mutual Life Insurance Company; Showa Shell Sekiyu K.K.; Yamadai Tetsusho Co., Ltd; Mr. Kotaro Terada; Sogo Bussan Co., Ltd, Japan Arts Council (Special Corporation)

Contractors
Takenaka Corporation/Obayashi Corporation; Kajima Corporation/Shimizu Corporation; Taisei Corporation/ Fujita Corporation; Odakyu Construction Co., Ltd; Kyoritsu Construction Co., Ltd; Keio Construction Co. Ltd/ Toda Corporation; Shoseki Engineering & Construction Co., Ltd

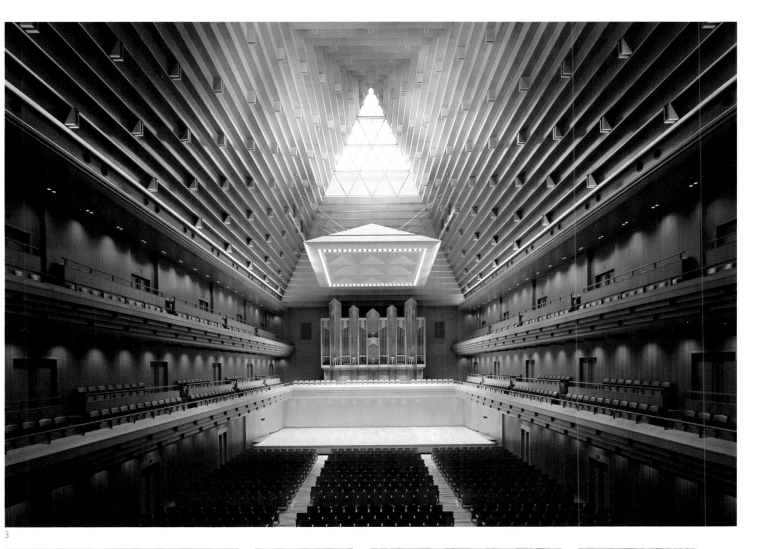

3

4

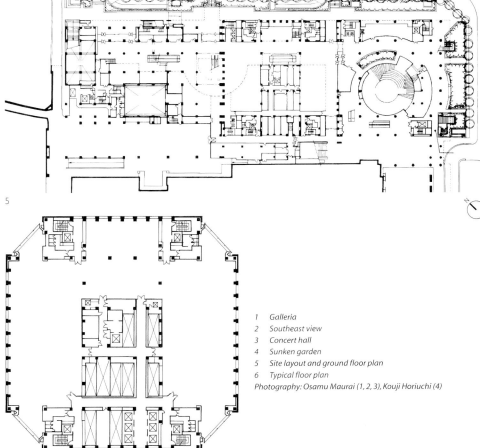

5

6

1   Galleria
2   Southeast view
3   Concert hall
4   Sunken garden
5   Site layout and ground floor plan
6   Typical floor plan
Photography: Osamu Maurai (1, 2, 3), Kouji Horiuchi (4)

Weihai CITIC Financial Building

■ This project stands 146.9 meters high; it has the sense of a magnificent and grand bank, together with a feeling of the unique background of the local culture. The main façade of the podium has been covered with local Shidao Hong granite. On top of both the main tower and the main entrance, unique shaped metal roofs have been built; this not only looks like a vulture with wings, but also a big silver ingot indicating the bank's prosperity in business.

In addition, it is the deformed shape of the upturned eaves and corbel bracket that reflects the established character of traditional national architecture, which is permeated with the unique charm of oriental architecture.

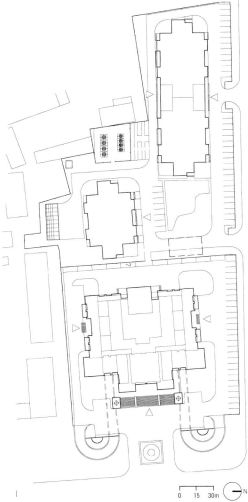

1

0   15   30m   N

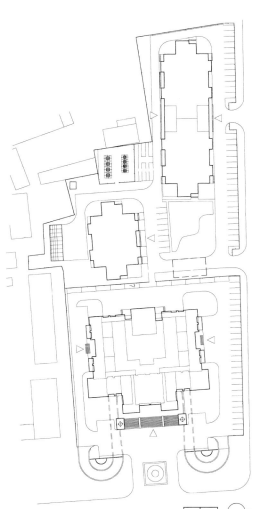

2

Location
Weihai, People's Republic of China

Completion
1998

Height
146.9 m

Stories
39 and 3 underground

Area
Building: 48,900 m²; site: 15,300 m²

Structure
Frame shear wall

Materials
Exterior: granite

Use
Bank, offices, hotel

Cost
330 million RMB

Architect
Architecture Design Institute Ministry of Construction

Client
CITIC Industrial Bank Weihai Branch

Contractor
2ⁿᵈ Bureau of CSCEC Weihai Branch Company

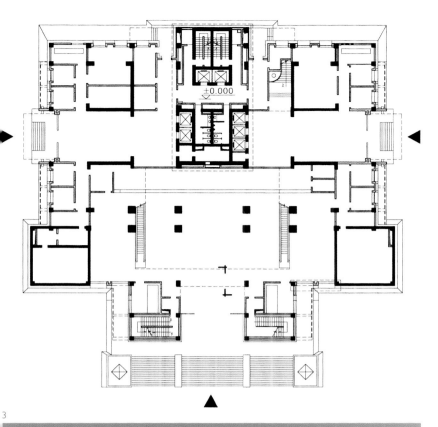

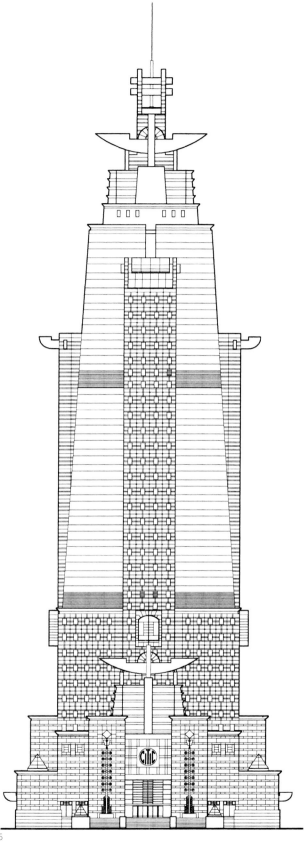

1 Site plan
2 Part view
3 Ground floor plan
4 Front view
5 Elevation
Photography: courtesy Architecture Design Institute Ministry
of Construction

Yuda World Trade Centre

■ Built on a 8,200 square meter site in the provincial Chinese city of Zhengzhou, this twin-towered structure includes a unified podium, 30 stories of separate offices linked by bridges at levels 15 and 30, and public observation, restaurant, and amenity facilities between levels 36 and 40.

Reaching a maximum height of 200 meters with a total of 125,000 square meters of gross serviced floor space, the structure of the building is reinforced concrete with combination cladding of two-color granite and tinted glass curtain walling. There are four basement floors containing extensive parking.

1

2

Location
Zhengzhou, People's Republic of China

Completion
1997

Height
200 m

Stories
40 and 4 basement

Area
Site: 8,200 m²; floor: 125,000 m²

Structure
Reinforced concrete

Materials
Granite, precast curtain wall

Use
Offices

Cost
US$110 million

Architect
C.Y. Lee & Partners, Architects & Planners

Client
Yuda Real Estate

3

4

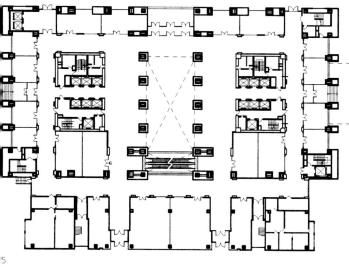

5

6

1   Front elevation
2   Side elevation
3   Podium detail
4   Canopy detail
5   First floor plan
6   Façade detail

Photography: courtesy C.Y. Lee & Partners, Architects & Planners

Buildings Recently Completed and Under Construction

206

11 Chater Road

Digital image: Advanced Media Design

This 900,000 square foot office tower is being developed by Hongkong Land in Central, Hong Kong. The site is bounded by Connaught Road, Pedder Street, and Chater Road. This mixed-use office and retail tower consists of three levels of below-grade parking, two levels of retail, a concourse level with four bridges connecting to adjacent properties, and a mezzanine level with restaurants. The new development will replace the existing Swire House and serve as a new focal point for the surrounding holdings of Hongkong Land.

The strong vertical gesture of the tower marks the corner of this prominent site. A semi-transparent vertical mass by day, the structure transforms into an urban lantern by night. The north and south façades respond to the dual context of the site as defined by the harbor and cityscape. The north façade faces the harbor where the curtain wall extends down to the street level. The south façade addresses the urban character of the city with a setback massing that is mediated by the pedestrian scaled retail podium. Two-story windows at the street level provide for maximum retail exposure and display of super-graphics.

Location
Hong Kong SAR, People's Republic of China

Completion
1999–2002

Height
134 m

Stories
27

Area
83,610 m²

Materials
Curtain wall: reflective silver glass and painted aluminum on glass and stone podium

Use
Offices and retail

Architect
Kohn Pedersen Fox Associates PC

Associate architect
LPT Architects

Structural engineer
Ove Arup & Partners

Service engineer
Flack + Kurtz

Client
Hongkong Land Ltd

Contractor
Gammon

1322 Roxas Boulevard

Digital image: Lawrence Leong & Phil Ishimaru

This 57-story luxury condominium will be located in one of Manila's best and most historical residential sites: on a corner property of Roxas Boulevard overlooking Rizal Park in the historic Ermita District on Manila Bay and the South China Sea.

The soaring tower will meet the sea like the rounded prow of a ship, slicing through the trade winds. The green, blue, and white glass façades will blend with the colors of the tropical seascape and landscape. The rounded forms of the structure and the profile of the top of the tower will recall the sails on a ship at sea. This nautical imagery will be further expressed in horizontal metal sunshades, which will protect the tower from glare and heat, while allowing outstanding views.

The bio-climatic nature of the tower is uniquely designed to take advantage of this specific site. The building orientation, with the narrowest profiles of the tower facing east and west and long façades to the north and south, supports efficient energy conservation. The building will provide operable windows to capture sea breezes and large window openings to maximize views, light, and air, with sunshades provided to minimize glare and heat.

At night, the tower lighting is designed to be a quiet beacon to identify what will be an important new landmark on Manila Bay.

Location
Manila, The Philippines

Completion
December 2001

Height
190 m; 203 m with spire

Stories
57

Area
111,000 m²

Structure
Concrete moment frame

Materials
Exterior: granite base with green-tinted glass and painted concrete; interior: marble and natural wood with bronze features

Use
Condominiums with amenities and retail

Architect
Architecture International, LTD

Associate architect
GF & Partners

Structural engineer
Aromin & Sy Associates, Ove Arup & Partners

Mechanical engineer
RJ Calpo & Partners

Client
Moldex Land, Inc.

Contractor
D.M. Consunji, Inc.

Beijing Tengda Building

Digital image: courtesy Architecture Design Institute Ministry of Construction

The Tengda Building will be situated at the crossing point between the Beijing city zone and the famous Zhong Guan Cun High-Tech Industrial Park (also called China's Silicon Valley) in the northwest suburb of Beijing. It will not only stand as the highest building on the west side of Beijing at 123 meters, but will also serve as a regional landmark together with provided culture facilities including the Purple Bamboo Park, the Beijing Zoo, and the Capital Gymnasium at the city main crossing.

The typical floor plan is made up of two right angle isosceles triangles inserted into a round. This, although somewhat strange, is a selection made to suit the surroundings while remaining simple and rational.

Location
Beijing, People's Republic of China

Completion
2000

Height
123 m

Stories
33

Area
Building: 86,800 m²; site: 10,000 m²

Structure
Frame shear wall

Materials
Exterior: glass curtain and aluminum panels

Use
Offices

Cost
400 million RMB

Architect
Architecture Design Institute Ministry of Construction

Client
Beijing Gaoling Real Estate Development Co. Ltd

Contractor
Beijing 4th City Construction Company

Daewoo Electronics Research and Development Headquarters

The design of this new research and development headquarters building is a challenging opportunity to inject some poetry into the prosaic office block and enhance the image of the Daewoo Corporation as a symbol of the city of Seoul and Korea. The proposed 166 meter high tower will accommodate 95,000 square meters of office and laboratory above ground, 10,000 square meters at lower ground level, and 50,000 square meters of parking and plant below ground level.

The profile of the skeletal form of this tapered slab tower has been likened to the hull of a traditional Korean ship, though in reality the shape optimizes the planning envelope regulations. The dramatic cantilevered rooftop helipad is elegantly idiosyncratic, suiting the building's role as a landmark for Seoul. The tower's structure will be a combination of steel and concrete. The main steel frame will be made up of two inner columns and two outer columns that follow the curved façade of the building. Steel outrigger trusses will provide stability at intervals up the structure. Where these occur, triple-height sky gardens will be created with the outside terraces. A slender steel and concrete central core will run the full height of the building distributing all services to the long, column-free office floors.

Photography: Tom Miller

Location
Seoul, Korea

Height
165 m

Stories
38

Area
Gross floor: 155,000 m²; aboveground: 96,000 m²

Structure
Steel frame with steel outrigger trusses

Materials
Concrete, steel, and glass

Use
Office, laboratory, plant, and parking

Architect
Foster and Partners

Collaborating architects
I&S Consortium

Structural engineer
Ove Arup & Partners

Mechanical and electrical engineer
Roger Preston & Partners

Client
Daewoo Electronics Co. Ltd

G.T. International Tower

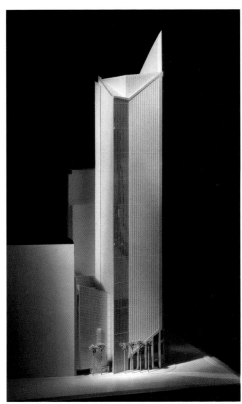

The G.T. International Tower was designed for a key site at the entry corner to Makati's primary commercial street, Ayala Avenue. The tower volume is composed of a series of taut glass planes which form a spiral, culminating in a faceted crown which marks the corner and forms the end of the avenue's street wall. This plane is lifted up at the building's base to reveal a plaza at the corner, where the structural columns emerge from beneath the tower's curtain wall to frame a canted plane at the third level. Visitors to the main lobby can view the activity at street level through this plane, which is located at the top of the lobby escalators.

The dominant surface of the tower is pulled away from the building's central volume at the intersection of Ayala Avenue and De La Costa Street, creating a vertical fissure in the tower's surface that provides a glimpse of the inner volume. A 10-story vertical fin marks the tower's presence on the Makati skyline and provides a visual signature at the tower's crown.

Photography: courtesy Kohn Pedersen Fox Associates PC

Location
Manila, The Philippines

Completion
Under construction

Height
217.2 m

Stories
43

Area
66,191 m²

Structure
Concrete

Materials
Reflective glass and aluminum curtain wall

Use
Offices

Architect
Kohn Pedersen Fox Associates PC

Associate architect
GF & Partners, Gozar Planners (HK) Ltd

Structural engineer
Ove Arup & Partners, Aromin & Sy Associates

Service engineer
R.J. Mojica & Partners, NBF Wastewater Services, R.J. Calpo & Partners

Client
Philippine Securities Corporation

Glorietta 4/The Oakwood

Photographer: Danny Feliciano

The Glorietta 4 hotel apartments is the newest addition to the 25-year evolution of an old city center, comprised of one- and two-story shops, into the contemporary 12.5 million square foot Ayala Center, a mixed-use development. A master plan established separate 'quads', each with its own mix of hotels, apartments, retail space, and feature parks. An unused outdoor space was covered to create a central 'Glorietta', linking each of the quads together.

It was Ayala Land's desire that the Glorietta 4, a 22-story hotel/apartment complex, provide a new signature identity for the center. The overall retail space of the center was expanded by adding five levels of restaurants, cinemas, high-end shops, and a food court. It was necessary to create an effective entrance/drop-off for the Glorietta 4 retail and hotel, and to also integrate the hotel/apartments with their park setting.

The landmark design for the Glorietta 4 will provide a unique skyscape—its lantern-effect lighting the sky at night, and providing a distinguishing identity during the day.

Location
Makati City, The Philippines

Completion
January 2000

Height
116 m

Stories
26

Area
Building: 102,00 m²; site: 13,000 m²

Structure
Concrete moment frame

Materials
Exterior: stone base granite, green-tinted glass, painted concrete; interior: natural wood trim and marble

Use
Hotel, apartments, retail, restaurants

Architect
Architecture International, LTD

Associate architect
GF & Partners

Structural engineer
E.H. Sison

Service engineer
DCDD Engineers

Client
Ayala Land, Inc., Ayala Hotels, Inc.

Contractor
D.M. Consunji, Inc.

Heyin Plaza

Digital image: courtesy Guangzhou Design Institute

Located on Huanshi East Road in Guangzhou, Heyin Plaza is a high-class office building. The plaza, together with the Guangzhou World Trade Center, the Garden Hotel, the Good World Plaza, and the Baiyun Hotel, form a large-scale city plaza. With its 56 stories, it is the highest building among the buildings nearby and occupies an important location. By utilizing the grade deference between Taojin Road and Huanshi East Road, the architect has rationally resolved the issue of the separation of pedestrian and vehicular traffic.

On floors two to 10 there is a bank business hall and other commercial service facilities; offices are located on the 13 floors above. The typical floor plan is in trapezium-shaped form, with three of four sides having slightly convex curves that form elegant building outlines.

The exterior of the building is covered with granite and a glass composite curtain wall. Heyin Plaza is a landmark building along the Huanshi East Road; its graceful vertical lines and step-down rooftop treatment distinguish the building from the surrounding buildings.

Location
Guangzhou, People's Republic of China

Completion
December 2000

Height
269.4 m

Stories
56

Area
131,792 m²

Structure
Framed tube-core structure, reinforced concrete core, steel core concrete column

Materials
Granite and glass composite curtain wall

Use
Offices

Cost
¥1200 million (RMB)

Architect
Guangzhou Design Institute

Structural engineer
Guangzhou Design Institute

Mechenical engineer
Guangzhou Design Institute

Client
Dapeng Group Inc.

Highcliff

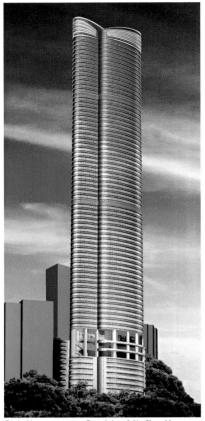

This development stands explicitly along No. 41D Stubbs Road. The harbor view, mountain, and trees are already in place. The architect Dennis Lau & Ng Chun Man Architects carefully plotted the development by not disturbing the natural terrain but allowing it to develop its individual interlocking elliptical identities.

Highcliff, a 73-story residential tower, consists of domestic units of sizes each approximately 255 square meters, a 265 square meter residents' clubhouse, ample carparking facilities, an outdoor swimming pool, and a beautiful external landscape.

To go with the interlocking elliptical residential block, each unit maximizes the view over Happy Valley and the Victoria Harbour. With an outstanding curtain wall design, each spacious residential unit is wrapped by floor-to-ceiling glazing that offers to integrate the panoramic view of nature with the interior.

The 17 meter high unique and distinctive all-glass cladding system at the podium highlights the emotion of the architect. The explicit glass elliptical staircase to the lower two levels' clubhouse area will be a unique experience. To make the most of the views, a multitude of exclusive facilities are offered in the clubhouse that will give the residents a feeling of luxury.

A special optical fiber lighting effect will twinkle up the signature roof features in the evening.

Digital image: courtesy Dennis Lau & Ng Chun Man Architects & Engineers (HK) Ltd

Location
Hong Kong SAR, People's Republic of China

Completion
August 2001

Height
252.3 m

Stories
73

Area
Site: 4,366 m²; gross floor: 34,928 m²

Structure
High-strength concrete consisting of composite work sequence, partially top-down and partially bottom-up method

Materials
External: curtain wall utilized system

Use
Deluxe high-rise residential development

Cost
US$128 million

Architect
Dennis Lau & Ng Chun Man Architects & Engineers (HK) Ltd

Structural engineer
Canwest Consultant (International) Ltd

Structural design consultant
Skilling Ward Magnusson Barkshire Inc.

Service engineer
Associated Consulting Engineers

Main contractor
Hip Hing Construction Co. Ltd

Client
Central Management Limited

International Finance Centre

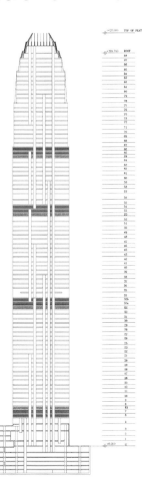

The International Finance Centre occupies one of the most beautiful urban sites in the world. It is located adjacent to the narrowest crossing of Victoria Harbour marking a new gateway to the city. This project reflects the importance of Hong Kong as a world financial center and will be an integral part of the new air terminal station, which offers express service to the new Chek Lap Kok Airport.

Phase One of the new development includes a 420 meter tall northeast office tower of approximately 181,000 square meters; a 210 meter tall southwest office tower of 73,000 square meters; and, a four story retail podium of 50,000 square meters with a public roof garden. Future phases of the development will include a hotel and service apartments.

The design of the northeast tower is in the tradition of true skyscrapers. It has a centric form that tapers with well-proportioned setbacks, expressing a vertical movement towards the sky. The massing of the tower becomes more sculptural near the top, enhancing this upward thrust. The surface articulation of the curtain wall reinforces the verticality of the design.

The top of the 420 meter tall northeast tower is designed as a welcoming gesture to the city. When lit at night, the sculptured tower top will shimmer like a pearl by Victoria Harbor.

Location
Hong Kong SAR, People's Republic of China

Completion
2002

Height
420 m

Stories
88

Area
181,000 m²

Materials
Curtain wall: lightly reflective glass panels and silver pearl-colored mullions

Architect
Rocco Design Ltd

Associated architect for station
Arup Associates

Design consultant for northeast tower
Cesar Pelli & Associates Inc.

Client
Central Waterfront Property Project Management Company Ltd

Kunming Construction Building

Photograph: courtesy Architecture Design Institute Ministry of Construction

Situated in the middle section of the Dong Feng East Road—the most important road in Kunming—this project will be a multi-functional building consisting of shops, a hostel, and commercial residences. The design has taken the contradictory situations between the city development and the environmental improvement into full consideration, and with the combination of the nature of the so-called 'Spring City's' climate, the design has placed emphasis on the architectural sustainability.

The plan has two rectangular shapes staggered together. This design has evenly laid intervals and paid attention to the contrast between vertical and horizontal lines on elevation, which are curling and straight in adequate proportion. The gray spaces of the building have been designed in harmony with the city landscape design.

Location
Kunming, People's Republic of China

Completion
2000

Height
106.9 m

Stories
26 and 2 underground

Area
53,400 m²

Structure
Frame shear wall

Materials
Interior: paint, tile; exterior: polished granite, concealed frame curtain wall, tile, aluminum frame with metal plating glass windows

Use
Commercial/office

Cost
141.15 million RMB

Architect
Architecture Design Institute Ministry of Construction

Client
Kunming City Construction Synthesize Development Company

Contractor
Kunming 2ⁿᵈ Construction Engineering Company

Landmark Tower

Digital image: courtesy Skidmore, Owings & Merrill LLP

SOM provided concept design for the 574 meter tall, 216,248 square meter Landmark Tower, which will be located at the MTRC land reclamation development site in Kowloon Bay. The multi-use building will be constructed on a podium over the new railway station and will consist of a hotel, commercial office building, retail areas, assembly components, and a carpark.

A multi-level restaurant and public observatory will be located at the top of the tower. Office space occupies the upper portion of the tower while a five-star hotel with a 23-story atrium will comprise the lower portion. A glass-enclosed circulation corridor on each floor will overlook the atrium space, providing access to guestrooms located on the building perimeter.

The podium portion of the project consists of executive parking accessible from the top of the podium; retail shops and public spaces; the observatory drop-off and entry; and loading dock facilities. Public access bridges to the adjacent southern and western areas are connected to the retail space of the tower. Five additional levels of parking will be located on basement levels below the podium. The tower parking facility will serve approximately 740 cars.

Location
Hong Kong SAR, People's Republic of China

Height
574 m

Stories
102

Area
Site: 8,900 m²; gross floor: 216,248 m²

Structure
Lateral load resisting system with eight composite steel and concrete megacolumns, two on each face of the tower, connected to a concrete shear wall core with steel outriggers located at each of the mechanical levels

Materials
Glass, stainless steel, aluminum, and granite

Use
Retail, luxury hotel, first-class office space, observation deck

Cost
Estimated in excess of US$500 million

Architect
Dennis Lau & Ng Chun Man Architects & Engineers (HK) Ltd in association with Skidmore, Owings & Merrill LLP

Structural engineer
Flack + Kurtz, New York

Services engineer
Daniel Chan & Associates Ltd, Hong Kong

Client
Mass Transit Development Corporation

Lite-On Technology Center

Photography: courtesy Artech Actchitects

This building is designed to be the headquarters of the Lite-On Groups company, a high-tech company with an annual income of US$50 million. The building will contain the executive office, general office, industrial working place, as well as the company's recreational center. The site is at a new computer industrial zone in Taipei City, bounded by mountains to the north and facing the Kee-long River to the south.

The base podium with a gentle slope will house the conference hall, training center, canteen, and staff recreation rooms. The entrance will be elevated to 5 meters in order to have the view of the river. The podium top garden will be fully planted and accompanied by water features, creating a promenade place, and with a view down the tower.

The architect has designed the building to mimic the smoothness and the solidity of the client's collection of china and jade. Small openings will be on the south, and large ones on north elevation.

The exterior cladding will be stone, metal, and glass. Empty areas on site will be planted with trees to give the impression that the building is growing in a forest.

Location
Taipei, Taiwan

Completion
2002

Height
107 m

Stories
23 and 4 below-grade

Area
69,775 m²

Structure
Structural steel

Materials
Granite, glass curtain wall

Use
Offices

Architect
Kris Yao/Artech Architects

Structural engineer
Ove Arup & Partners

Mechanical engineer
I.S. Lin Associates, Architects and Engineers

Client
Lite-On Groups

Construction Manager
Taiwan Real Estate Management Group

Lujiazui-Itochu Building

Digital image: The Drawing Studio

Sydness Architects was awarded this commission after winning an international design competition that included architects from Japan, Germany, Great Britain, and the United States.

The owners are the Lujiazui Development Company of Shanghai and Itochu, a Japanese multinational company. They will both occupy the building as headquarters at the heart of the Lujiazui Finance and Trade Zone in the Pudong area of Shanghai.

The building's form is a response to the configuration of the site and to its location on a prominent corner. The plan is two semicircles that are shifted along the diameter to fit snugly within the property lines. The building is then modified in deference to standard office modules and building products and has a serrated edge on a shifting 1.2 meter module.

The undulating perimeter curtain wall of flamed and polished granite is accented by granite vertical ribs that rise up the tower to a stepped top that echoes the plan against the sky.

The lower floors are clad with horizontal stone mullions and gray vision glass and spandrel glass. A large plaza facing southwest leads to a recessed circular glazed entry. Occupancy is expected in 2000.

Location
Shanghai, People's Republic of China

Completion
2001

Height
122 m

Stories
28

Area
Building: 51,500 m²

Structure
Poured-in-place concrete

Materials
Granite, glass, aluminum, and bronze

Use
Corporate headquarters, commercial office

Cost
US$60 million

Architect
Sydness Architects, P.C.

Associate architect
Shanghai Institute of Architectural Design and Research

Structural engineer
Leslie E. Robertson Associates

Services
M.E.P. Design Consultants, Flack + Kurtz

Client
Lujiazui-Itochu Development Building Co., Ltd

Muromachi Mitsui Shinkan Building

Digital image: courtesy Cesar Pelli & Associates Inc.

Following an invited design competition, Mitsui-Fudosan, one of Japan's largest real estate firms, recently selected Cesar Pelli & Associates to design this new 41-story mixed-use tower that will include corporate offices for the Mitsui Group as well as trading floors and luxury retail components. It will be located in Muromachi, one of the most historically significant areas of Tokyo, with panoramic views of Tokyo Bay, adjacent to the landmark Mitsui Main Building—the 1929 Neoclassical Sakura Bank designed by Trow Bridge and Livingston, Architects.

Location
Tokyo, Japan
Completion
2007
Height
188 m
Stories
41
Area
130,000 m²
Architect
Cesar Pelli & Associates Inc.
Client
Mitsui-Fudosan Co., Ltd

Nakanoshima Mitsui Building

Digital image: courtesy Cesar Pelli & Associates Inc.

Following an invited design competition, Cesar Pelli & Associates was recently selected by Mitsui-Fudosan, one of Japan's largest real estate firms, to design this new office tower, which will be situated on a prominent site on the island of Nakanoshima in central Tokyo. Fronting on both the Tosabori and Dojima rivers, this 31-story building will serve as headquarters to several companies of the Mitsui Group.

The Nakanoshima Mitsui Building is slated to be the highest office tower on the Nakanoshima island.

Location
Osaka, Japan
Height
140 m
Stories
31
Area
75,000 m²
Architect
Cesar Pelli & Associates Inc.
Client
Mitsui-Fudosan Co., Ltd

Plaza 66

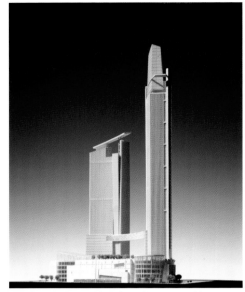

Digital image: courtesy Kohn Pedersen Fox Associates PC

The Nanjing Xi Lu project, currently under construction, is situated along the busiest commercial street in Shanghai's central district. The program calls for a mix of 59,084 square meters of retail and 139,350 square meters of office space. The retail has been configured as a five-story podium, matching the scale of the historical Chinese streetscape, and is punctuated by two major interior public spaces. The towers, which contain office space in floorplates of roughly 1,765 square meters, are entered separately from the rear of the site.

While the street level entrance separates the major functions, the massing creates a unified composition. The curved volumes of the base are cradled by the tower walls, which spiral in ascending fashion to the top of the 60-story tower. At its apex of 244.7 meters, the complex is punctuated by a lantern formed of billowing screens which will glow at night over the city.

Location
Shanghai, People's Republic of China

Completion
2001

Height
244.7 m

Stories
60

Area
295,422 m²

Use
Mixed-use building: office and retail

Client
Hang Lung Development Co., Ltd

Architect
Kohn Pedersen Fox Associates PC

Associate architect
Frank C.Y. Feng Architects and Associates (HK) Ltd

Scotts Tower

Photography: courtesy Ong & Ong Architects

This 23-story, 91 meter high apartment building has a plan that is mostly elliptical, except for one side that houses its elevator and staircase core. Its façade is defined by a number of interlocking elliptical bodies that recall the dynamic designs of early twentieth century architects such as Erich Mendelsohn and members of the Bauhaus. The lower half of the tower is defined by horizontal ribbon windows that are set in wide, protruding frames and wrap around the building's corner. Aluminum fins at the shifting of the ellipse function as visual extensions of these horizontal components. On top of the tower, the mechanical plant is hidden behind elliptical louvers which are, in turn, crowned by a metal-clad, hyperbolic plane that is pierced by a mast. With its striking architectural forms and full-height, blue-tinted glass windows, the Scotts Tower vividly invokes the streamlined design favored by architects at the beginning of the twentieth-century.

Location
Singapore, Republic of Singapore

Completion date
November 2001 (targeted)

Height
91 m

Stories
23

Area
3,040 m²

Materials
Curtain walling system combining glass and an external pre-formed panel

Use
Residential

Cost
S$30 million

Architect
Ong & Ong Architects Private Limited

Structural engineer
Steen Consultants Pte Ltd

Mechanical and electrical engineer
Alpha Engineering Consultant

Client
Far East Organization

Main contractor
Poh Lian Construction Pte Ltd

Shanghai Information Center Building

Photography: courtesy Nikken Sekkei Ltd

This 41-story building will be an integrated office complex consisting of a telecommunication and information museum, regional telecommunication equipment rooms, administration offices, and office space for tenants.

As the project site is located in the center part of the Pudong Development area and faces the 100 meter wide main road of the region, the design solution called for a form that would represent a gateway tower for this area. Because there are four high-rise towers over 100 meters on this block, the theme is to create a highly symbolic and unified building for the multiple functions in addition to creating a comfortable public space against the wall of soaring high-rise buildings.

To demonstrate this design theme, a twin core system has been adopted, which enables a wider integration of various kinds of service shafts rather than a typical center core system. This scheme was developed into a rigid frame structure with super transfer truss beams at three levels in the center.

The design of the façade of the main telecommunication machine area at the middle of the tower is emphasized by horizontal strips of continuous window and aluminum spandrel while the upper half is clad by half mirror glass curtain wall skin.

Location
Shanghai, People's Republic of China

Scheduled completion
December 2000

Height
180 m

Stories
41, 4 basements, 2 penthouses

Area
Site: 8,250 m²; building: 2,200 m²; total floor: 93,000 m²

Structure
Steel encased in reinforced concrete, reinforced concrete, steel frame

Use
Mixed use, including museum, telecommunication equipment rooms, offices

Architect
Nikken Sekkei Ltd

Engineer
Nikken Sekkei Ltd

Client
Shanghai Pudong International World Co., Ltd

Shanghai World Financial Center

Photography: courtesy Kohn Pedersen Fox Associates PC

When it is completed, the Shanghai World Financial Center will stand as the tallest building in the world. The project is located on a key site in the Lujiazhui financial and trade district in Pudong, which the Chinese government has designated as an Asian center for international banking and commercial interests.

The program of this 95-story project is contained within two distinctly formal elements: a sculpted tower and podium, corresponding to the ancient Chinese conception of the earth as a square and the sky as a circle. The union between these geometric forms gives shape to the tower transforming it into a symbolic repository invested with resonances particular to the culture and cosmology of China.

The primary form of the tower is devised as a square prism intersected by two sweeping arcs, tapering into a single line at the apex. The gradual progression of floor plans generates configurations which are ideal for offices on the lower floors and hotel suites above. At the same time, the transformation of the plan rotates the orientation of the upper portion of the tower with the oriental pearl TV tower, the area's dominant landmark, a fifth of a mile away. To relieve wind pressure, a 50 meter cylinder is carved out of the top of the building. Equal in diameter to the sphere of the television tower, this void connects the two structures. Penetrating through and surrounding the massive stone base of the tower are wall, wing, and conical forms.

Location
Shanghai, People's Republic of China

Height
460 m

Stories
95

Area
312,144 m²

Materials
Tower shaft: glass curtain wall with horizontal stainless steel fins; base: granite with cleft finish; podium forms: clear glass cladding with stainless steel mullions, honed granite, and metal panels

Use
Mixed use: office, luxury hotel (300 rooms), retail, gallery, and observation deck

Architect
Kohn Pedersen Fox Associates PC

Associate architect
Mori Building Architects & Engineers; East China Architectural Design and Research Institute

Structural engineer for schematic design
Ove Arup

Mechanical engineer
Mori Building Architects and Engineers

Contractor
I. P. Construction

Shiodome Office Buildings and Retail (Block B)

Digital image: courtesy Kevin Roche John Dinkeloo and Associates

Shiodome Block B is an irregular-shaped site, facing on the north side is a network of streets and elevated roadways, on the east and south sides as yet unfinalized large high-rise projects, and on the west side an undistinguished low-rise development. The project is complicated by the central location of the old Shimbashi Station. Many scale models were studied of the proposed AM Office Tower and the Matsushita Headquarters, which will occupy the most prominent position of the site because of its smaller size.

In order to take advantage of the views to the southeast of the Hamarikyu Gardens and harbor, and to the northwest of the central business district and the Palace Gardens, the building was rotated on the site. This rotation also allows for the best exposure from Express Highway No. 1, but the rotated rectangular buildings did not relate satisfactorily either to the Shimbashi Station or to the adjacent developments. A number of different plan configurations were explored and finally a curved plan form was selected as the one that gave the best overall visual results and the ideal urban design solution.

Location
Tokyo, Japan

Completion
January 2003

Height
215 m

Stories
43

Area
190,000 m²

Structure
Steel

Materials
Glass, aluminum, granite

Use
Commercial

Architect
Kevin Roche John Dinkeloo and Associates

Associate architect
Nihon Sekkei, Inc.

Structural engineer
Nihon Sekkei, Inc.

Service engineer
Nihon Sekkei, Inc.

Client
Alderney Investment Group (GIC), Matsushita Electric Co., Mitsui Fudosan Co., Ltd

Contractor
Takenaka Corporation

St Regis Hotel

Photography: Justin Van Soest

The St Regis Hotel in Shanghai will be a five-star international hotel that will be operated by Starwood Hotels and Resorts as a member of their exclusive Luxury Collection. The hotel, which will be located in the Pudong New Area, is 38 stories with 385 rooms, a lounge and restaurant at the top, and a 24 meter high podium that contains the essential hotel functions including a three-story lobby, ballroom, five restaurants, fitness center, conference facilities, and retail spaces.

The slender tower will be clad in red granite expressed in a grid that responds to the guestroom module and the story height. The gently curving peaks at the top of the tower will be set at different heights and point in opposite directions, while a glass-enclosed central corridor sandwiched between the stone-clad slabs will rise up and allow expansive views of the city from a restaurant and lounge located at the top.

Sydness Architects was commissioned for the project after winning an international design competition involving four firms.

Location
Shanghai, People's Republic of China

Completion
2001

Height
148.5 m

Stories
38

Area
Building: 50,000 m²

Structure
Poured-in-place concrete

Materials
Exterior: granite, glass, and aluminum; interior: granite, marble, and wood

Use
Hospitality

Cost
US$60 million

Architect
Sydness Architects, P.C.

Associate architect
East China Architectural Design Institution

Structural engineer
Leslie E. Robertson Associates

Services
M.E.P. Design Consultants, Flack + Kurtz

Client
Starwood Hotels & Resorts

Taichung Tower II

Digital image: courtesy Kohn Pedersen Fox Associates PC

The design for Taichung Tower II, set on a prominent site at the end of a kilometer-long stretch of park in Taichung, Taiwan, was inspired not only by its physical context but also by the cultural context suggested through the symbolism of hidden meaning. These influences inspire a building of poetic simplicity.

The building takes a bold sculptural form that curves on two sides, responding to open park views as well as to the oblique approach from the Taichung-Kang Road to the northeast. The building curves as it rises, beginning with large lobby, ballroom, and restaurant floor plates, and narrows as it moves to the smaller hotel room, and office suite plates at the top. The structure thus becomes two 'shell' forms, curving in two directions to create a simple yet dramatic profile on the skyline. The exterior wall panels remain basic rectangular shapes, with all dimensional variation taken up in the panel joints.

The hotel is housed in the mid-level floors of the tower. The 300-room Intercontinental hotel offers full amenities including convention and ballroom space, as well as convenient access to services on the lower levels.

In developing this design, the architect discovered that the tower plan suggested the form of a fish. After researching some of the calligraphic origins of Chinese symbolism, it was recognized that the image of a fish facing east is interpreted in Taiwan as good fortune. This image had significant meaning to the client, so it continued to be incorporated and further developed throughout the design process.

Location
Taichung, Taiwan
Completion
1996–2001
Height
175 m
Stories
27
Area
4,923 m²
Materials
Exterior: aluminum and glass curtain wall, stainless steel, granite, glass; interior: stone, wood panels, glass, stainless steel, bronze
Use
Hotel and offices
Architect
Kohn Pedersen Fox Associates PC
Associate architect
Chang & Jan. Architects & Planners
Structural engineer
Federal Engineering
Mechanical engineer
Continental Engineering
Client
Tzung Tang Development Group
Contractor
CCC Construction, Taichung

Taipei Financial Center

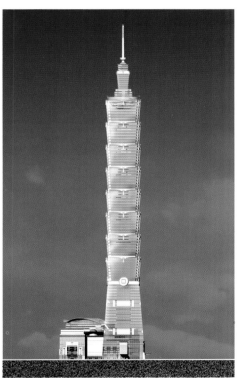

Digital image: courtesy C.Y. Lee & Partners

To promote Taiwan in the Asia-Pacific, the government has provided public land located in the golden section of the Hsin-yee financial district in order to speed up building in the Taipei financial center.

With the creative urban street as the core, various movement lines emit in radius to form a network. Diversified urban spaces are connected by taking advantage of the air corridor, ground pedestrian walkways, an open-space system, and an underground pedestrian movement line.

Beginning with the idea of an inward inclined observation deck, the Taipei Financial Center has eight floors as platforms, with all these platforms interlocked and interacting to exhibit dynamite vitality. The blooming petal-like structure will soar into the sky to symbolize the image of the 'upgrading and fullness' of Chinese culture and prosperous economic power. The clean-cut and powerful silhouette of the high-rise will provide a new skyline and a new landmark for the city of Taipei. The building is a good example of the utilization of high-tech and energy-saving efficiency; the Taipei Financial Center will use transparent vitreous materials and innovative lighting design. This super high-rise will pave the way for Taiwan in the new era.

Location
Taipei, Taiwan
Completion
October 2002
Stories
101 and 5 basements
Area
Site: 30,277 m²
Use
Offices
Architect
C.Y. Lee & Partners
Land owner
Taipei City Government

Tangshan Xinhua Building

Digital image: courtesy Architecture Design Institute Ministry of Construction

The project site is quite narrow; it has a three-story hotel at the south side and a 55 meter high, 50 meter wide microwave corridor running obliquely across the site at the east. With these disadvantages in mind, the concept design has been done so as to put the tower at the west side of the site and to form a 60 degree triangle element within the included angle formed between the corridor and the site. As a result, an oblique city landscape belt has been formed all the way from the city central square to the southwest of the site, to the Phoenix Hill Park on the northeast until Da Cheng Hill Park. The oblique elements of the project make it mingle into these scenes. Furthermore, the arched metal glass structure placed in an oblique manner strengthens this relationship. The two wings of the tower form a huge vertical gray space that opens to the podium that encloses a courtyard. It forms an abundant inward view that makes people feel the interchange of indoor and outdoor public spaces.

Location
Tangshan, People's Republic of China
Completion
2000
Height
82.23 m
Stories
22 and 2 underground
Area
Building: 18,800 m²; site: 5,400 m²
Structure
Frame/shear wall
Materials
Interior: stone, carpet, paint; exterior: red tile, paint, dark color metal curtain wall
Use
Hotel
Cost
80 million RMB
Architect
Architecture Design Institute Ministry of Construction
Contractor
The 22nd Metallurgical Construction Company of China

Tomorrow Square Marriott

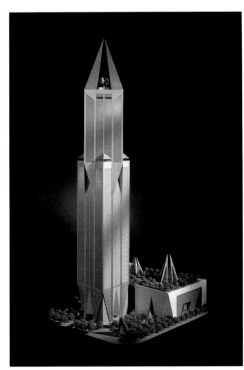

Digital image: courtesy John Portman & Associates

Tomorrow Square symbolizes Shanghai's future: dynamic, sophisticated, contemporary, and futuristic. Strategically located on Nanjing Road adjacent to People's Park, Tomorrow Square has an unmatched opportunity to create a powerful visual impact. The sleek 55-story tower is clad in aluminum and glass. Reaching upward in a straightforward, geometric manner, the building boasts clean and uncluttered lines with the contemporary look of the future. The building's vertical movement is reinforced by the dominant triangular shapes at both the top and base. This impact is increased by the placement of the tower—it rises directly from a landscaped plaza at street level, facing two of the major streets that border the site.

There are two main structures: the tower and podium. The tower, originally designed as a hotel and office building, is now being renovated to a business class, 500-room hotel, and business apartments complex for JW Marriott. The podium includes the low-rise retail galleria and conference center. To reinforce its strong vertical form, the tower and podium are visually separate though functionally linked via a skylit atrium.

Pedestrian and vehicular circulation were planned to make the activities within the site easily accessible, including clearly defined motor access to the entrances for the hotel and shops. The landscaped plazas, rooftop gardens, and pools provide park-like settings in an urban environment, offering a reprise from the congestion of the city.

Location
Shanghai, People's Republic of China
Completion
2001
Height
280 m
Stories
55
Area
93,153 m²
Structure
Reinforced concrete
Materials
Aluminum, glass curtain wall, granite
Use
Hotel, retail, conference
Cost
$125 million
Architect
John Portman & Associates
Structural engineer
John Portman & Associates (aka: AES)
Service engineer
Newcomb & Boyd Engineering
Client
Shanghai Sunjoy Real Estate General Co.
Contractor
Timalco International Pty Ltd

Wan Xiang International Plaza

Illustration: Peter Wels, Hamburg

The Wang Xiang International Plaza project is located in the center of Shanghai. The land is immediately adjacent to Nanjing Road, China's largest shopping street and to Xiang Road, the main north-south traffic route.

The design concept is based on four independent architectural elements: the 250 meter tower; the 10-story, 48 meter retail center with an arcade as a linear connection between buildings and the external link to the footway network; and finally, the loggia over the plaza, enclosing the space.

The design acknowledges the significance of the Wan Xiang International Plaza in relation to the totality of Shanghai's town planning structure.

The skywalk at the intersection directly connects with the arcade at the mezzanine floor level. The arcade connects the 10-story shopping center with two panoramic elevators and moving stairways. The story-high glazed façade is semi-transparent—adjustable interior screens and fixed features behind the façade ensure the appropriate degree of shade for the shopping areas.

The most impressive characteristic of the building is the way the structural frame fits behind the smooth, totally glass façade. The positioning and size of the diagonals and the connections emphasize the design concept and take into account the effects of forces arising from earthquakes.

The façade encapsulating the building and separating the interior and exterior spaces is a twin-skinned story-high glazed ventilation façade.

Location
Shanghai, People's Republic of China

Height
242.78 m (excluding mast); 318.88 m (including mast)

Stories
52

Area
Plan: 9,413,30 m²; building: 4,731,00 m²; total floor: 91,600 m²

Architect
Ingenhoven Overdiek und Partner, Düsseldorf

Contact architects, Shanghai
East China Architectural Design & Research Institute

Structural engineers
Büro Happold, Bath

Technical engineers
RCI, Rudolf Otto Meyer Consult International, Düsseldorf

Client
Shanghai Wan Xiang International Plaza Company Ltd

Contractor
Construction Group No.1 Shanghai

Xian Hi-Tech International Business Center

Digital image: Phil Ishimaru

The Xian Hi-Tech International Business Center is a 131,000 square meter mixed-use development, which includes office and residential towers, and three levels of flexible retail space. A landmark design for a semi-circular office tower encourages the sweep of pedestrians from adjacent thoroughfares into the plaza. Retail shops are located along this walk leading to a large department store and atrium at the center of the complex. Special care is taken in the orientation of the residential tower to take advantage of views and the southern exposure. Internal open residential corridors encourage air circulation into the building's core and help regulate temperatures.

The rounded architectural forms of the towers and the curved forms of the lower level podium at the base, will become a symbol of the complex. These distinctive forms, together with the unique profile of the towers on the skyline, will become the identity signature of this complex. From the east and from the south, the rounded towers establish the image of the complex. From the north and the west, the predominantly rectilinear forms of the towers are in harmony with the other towers in the district.

Location
Xian, People's Republic of China

Completion
Spring 2002

Height
Office tower: 140 m (150 m with spire); residential tower: 100 m

Stories
Office tower: 36; residential tower: 30

Area
131,000 m²

Structure
Concrete frame

Materials
Stone, glass, and metal

Use
Headquarters office, residential and retail shops, and plaza open to public

Architect
Architecture International, LTD

Associate architect
Concept International Consulting Group

Structural/Service engineer
Northwest Design Institute

Client
Xian High-Tech Industries Group Co. Ltd

Index
Architects

Index
Buildings
(Organized alphabetically by location)

Acknowledgments

IMAGES is pleased to present 'Tall Buildings of Asia and Australia', to its compendium of design and architectural publications.

We wish to thank all participating firms for their valuable contribution to this publication.

Our special thanks to Georges Binder, Buildings & Data s.a., for the invaluable research material provided.